T0268514

REPRESENT

REPRESENT

THE UNFINISHED FIGHT FOR THE VOTE

MICHAEL ERIC DYSON
& MARC FAVREAU

LITTLE, BROWN AND COMPANY
New York   Boston

Little, Brown and Company
Hachette Book Group
1290 Avenue of the Americas, New York, NY 10104
Visit us at LBYR.com

First Edition: September 2024

Little, Brown and Company is a division of Hachette Book Group, Inc. The Little, Brown name and logo are registered trademarks of Hachette Book Group, Inc.

The publisher is not responsible for websites (or their content) that are not owned by the publisher.

Little, Brown and Company books may be purchased in bulk for business, educational, or promotional use. For information, please contact your local bookseller or the Hachette Book Group Special Markets Department at special.markets@hbgusa.com.

Library of Congress Cataloging-in-Publication Data
Names: Dyson, Michael Eric, author. | Favreau, Marc, 1968– author.
Title: Represent : the unfinished fight for the vote /
Michael Eric Dyson and Marc Favreau.
Description: First edition. | New York : Little, Brown and
Company, [2024] | Includes bibliographical references and index. |
Summary: "An exploration of the ongoing fight for democracy in
the United States, from the American Revolution to the present day."
—Provided by publisher.
Identifiers: LCCN 2023053323 | ISBN 9780759557062
(hardcover) | ISBN 9780759557055 (ebook)
Subjects: LCSH: Democracy—United States—History—Juvenile
literature. | Political participation—United States—Juvenile literature.
Classification: LCC JK1726 .D97 2024 |
DDC 323/.0420973—dc23/eng/20240506
LC record available at https://lccn.loc.gov/2023053323

ISBNs: 978-0-7595-5706-2 (hardcover),
978-0-7595-5705-5 (ebook)

Printed in Virginia, USA

LSC-H

Printing 3, 2024

This is to the memories of my wonderful
aunt Mary Leonard and her daughter,
Barbara Ann Jenkins, my beloved cousin.
—Michael

This is for Owen and Emmett, all grown up
but still my buddy boys.
—Marc

The ultimate end of all freedom is the enjoyment of a right of free suffrage.[1]

—"A WATCHMAN," *Maryland Gazette*, 1776

We are not helpless. The fire is still burning. Please go out and vote this November. So many people have died and sacrificed so much for us to have our voice, we have to use it. Use our voices to do something great for our children.

—Beyoncé, 2016

[1] Suffrage, *noun*—the right to vote. *Oxford English Dictionary*

CONTENTS

PART 3: TWO ROADS

A NOTE TO READERS

YOUR FREEDOM IS IN DANGER.

Wait—did you read that correctly?

You bet you did.

It's in danger because some people—very powerful people—are trying to make sure that we Americans don't vote. Others are working overtime to make sure that when we do vote, it won't matter anyway. It's all part of a plan.

And it's just the latest chapter in the long story of American democracy, which is the story of a struggle between those who want the people to have power and those who don't.

In the last few years, that contest has come to a head. An American president tried to overturn the results of an election and block the peaceful transfer of power. The US Capitol was attacked by a violent mob. And then many powerful people did their best to deny that any of this ever happened. Except it's the stone-cold truth.

All of a sudden, the survival of our democracy may well depend on the difference between truth and lies. How we define some of the oldest words in the American political vocabulary—*democracy, voting, equality*—matters more than ever.

Democracy is easy: It means "people power."

Democracy is supposed to be as American as apple pie. The truth is, *democracy* is not a word that rolled off the tongues of the Founding Fathers, and that's because many of them feared what might happen if all kinds of people could vote. It has been up to the people—people like us—to claim that voting power for ourselves.

Voting is a centuries-old term. A vote is a wish or a vow.

What are your wishes, your desires? What kind of society do you wish to live in? How do you make your wishes real? There are many different ways for you to express your wishes and desires. But in a democracy, there is no way more powerful than voting.

Equality comes from a root meaning "level" or "even."

In our democracy, voting is how we achieve equality, because it puts all people on the same level footing. Our freedom depends on each of us, equally, having access to this simple tool.

A NOTE TO READERS

For 250 years, people just like you stepped forward to tell their truths and to fight for their wishes and desires for a different world. The heroes of this story are not the usual suspects from your history class. They include a fugitive slave, a Chinese American teenager, a Lakota Sioux activist, a poor sharecropper, a Mexican American student, and others. All of them put everything on the line for their right to vote.

Represent tells a story about the fight for people power in America: the fight for all Americans to be counted equally as citizens, and to make their voices heard.

Of the true stories that make up our common history, the quest for representation is the most electrifying, the most passionate, and the least understood. The real story of voting in America is about an epic quest, by some of the most interesting (and often little-known) heroes our country has produced, to build the democracy that was sketched out in the Constitution but remains unfinished in the twenty-first century.

It's a story that belongs to all of us.

Michael Eric Dyson and Marc Favreau
October 2023

A ballot box from Deptford Township, New Jersey, 1811, with an inscription meaning "voice of the people."

GLOUCESTER COUNTY HISTORICAL SOCIETY

Prologue

WHOSE REVOLUTION?

FIFTY-FIVE MEN, HUNKERED DOWN BEHIND CLOSED DOORS, had to pull off something in four months that had not been attempted in any other country in all human history. In 1787, representatives from the thirteen American states gathered in Philadelphia to draft the United States Constitution, a blueprint of laws for a new nation. They had few examples to guide them. They disagreed more than they agreed. An entire nation, many of whose citizens had risked their lives to make this day possible, was breathing down their necks.

These men knew they had to get the job done.

Week in, week out, the debates raged, and at times disagreement threatened to scuttle their efforts.

They were certain of one thing, however: They could not establish a true democracy. The US Constitution could not give *all* the people power.

Why not?

Nearly *half* of the fifty-five men who met to draft the Constitution owned other human beings. While they toiled in Philadelphia, these Founding Fathers utterly depended on the forced labor of other people for their own livelihoods. They had no intention of freeing the more than 700,000 men, women, and children (about one-fifth of the entire population!) who remained in bondage in the United States.

African American people, both enslaved and free, perfectly understood what was at stake. During the American Revolution, thousands of them had run away from their enslavers—taking the promises of the Declaration of Independence at face value. Thousands more had fought in the war for freedom from Great Britain and returned home on equal footing with all patriots. Their liberty was infectious.

"We are endowed with the same Faculties [as] our masters," two enslaved men petitioned the Connecticut state legislature, "and the more we Consider of this matter, the more we are Convinced of our Right...to be free."

The Constitution dashed these hopes. The new nation would be a place where slavery thrived, instead of disappeared.

With the question of slavery out of the way, the framers *still* had to figure out what to do about the rest of the population.

Who would have power in this brand-new country? Who would get to decide?

And rather than settle this issue once and for all, the framers did something unexpected with that burning question of representation, the very thing that had sparked the epic fight to gain independence from Great Britain in the first place. Instead of insisting on the last word, they let the states decide who could vote and who could not. There would be no single rule written into the Constitution. For most of the next century, each state made a different call on this all-important question—a fact with dire consequences for the American majority.

The framers might have believed they had performed a kind of magic trick in Philadelphia by making the problem of inequality disappear. But the truth is that they made sure that the Revolution had not really ended and that Americans would be fighting for representation for the next 237 years and more.

The irony of our history is that the original United States Constitution, the blueprint of our democracy, did not actually give Americans the right to vote—the very thing that defines democracy in the first place.

In the beginning, with independence, a new constitution, and thirteen states, here's where things stood:

- Only a small handful of women could vote—and only in one single state. The New Jersey Constitution, passed in 1776, specifically referred to voters as "they," which meant men *and* women. Fourteen years later, state legislators went even further, referring to legal voters as "he or she." No other state in the young nation had singled out women as having the right to vote.

- Most states kept property requirements (especially ownership of land or real estate) for voting, which meant that even the majority of men—sailors, carpenters, dockworkers, blacksmiths, and even soldiers—remained unrepresented in the new government.

- All states treated Native Americans like outsiders or foreigners—to be negotiated with or invaded and defeated.

◆   Some states allowed free Black people to
    vote, but others prohibited them from cast-
    ing ballots.

In all, approximately one-third of the population could
vote. Who could call that a democracy?

None of this was a secret to any person living in the
new United States. Those people left out felt the sting of
exclusion—and those people on the inside feared what
might happen if the majority was let in.

The American majority—women, African Americans,
Native Americans—would have no say in their country's
future, or their own lives. Their own country denied them
representation as equals.

The first generation of Americans quickly learned just
how precarious, how uncertain, their access to voting
could be.

In 1807, without warning, men shut the door on
women voters in New Jersey. "Be it enacted," a new law
said, that "no person shall vote in any state or county election for officers in the government of the United States, or
of this state, unless such person be a free, white, male citizen of this state." In the next year's elections, not a single

woman could cast her vote. Women could not vote again in New Jersey for more than one hundred years.

Women in New Jersey learned a bitter truth about America's shaky experiment in representation: No one could take it for granted. Ever.

(In the years following, the women of New Jersey—far from giving up—laid the foundation for a new generation, establishing schools and other educational institutions for girls. Many of these same girls grew up to become suffragists, carrying the fight to vote forward in a new era.)

The experience of the Revolutionary era, of hopes and disappointments, taught the majority of Americans that nothing came for free and that no one would simply hand them a seat at democracy's table. They already knew in their bones what it meant to be on the outside.

As the new century dawned, the long fight for people power was on.

Part One

PROMISES

THE FOUNDING FATHERS HAD DECIDED WHO WAS in, and who was out. With so few people allowed to vote, the big questions posed by the Revolution—about equality, freedom, and democracy—retreated to the sidelines.

After a brief but bloody war with Great Britain in 1812, many Americans seemed to put aside their differences and to celebrate the simple fact of being "American." The years that followed, sometimes called the Era of Good Feelings, confirmed for them that the nation was on the right track.

But beneath a calm surface, bad feelings began to bubble up among people on the outside. That's because the Founders hadn't counted on the power of their own words, which had a way of echoing far beyond their authors' original intentions. Overheard in speeches, passed down from parents to children, studied in pamphlets, posters, and books, ideas about equality and democracy kept freedom dreams alive.

The County Election by the painter George Caleb Bingham is one of the most famous attempts to depict the excitement of white male suffrage in the Jacksonian era.

Chapter One

EQUALITY?

IN THE FALL OF 1831, A FRENCH WRITER NAMED ALEXIS de Tocqueville returned home from a nine-month journey to the United States. He explored the young nation, making observations and jotting down notes about the political habits of American citizens. He published his writings as a book, *Democracy in America*, which quickly became a hit in France—a much older nation, which was struggling with its own shaky experiment in political equality.

America, he discovered, was a place where the ideal of equality ran deep, even when the reality of *inequality*, between rich and poor, enslaved and free, and women and men, was everywhere to see.

According to de Tocqueville, ordinary, hardworking men prized their status as equal members of American society (only men could claim this prize) even when they had no money or property. They had self-respect and tended to make fun of the pretensions of the rich and famous—or anyone, really, who tried to act superior to them. The simple act of shaking hands told de Tocqueville everything he needed to know about American values, because it symbolized a desire to be acknowledged, and to acknowledge others, as free and equal citizens.

But what it meant to be free and equal in America in the 1830s was changing, fast.

By the time de Tocqueville arrived on its shores, the America of the American Revolution—a place of farms, small craftsmen, and plantations—had been shaken to its core by a market revolution. Instead of producing crops and goods for themselves or their local communities, more people now bought what they needed and sold what they produced, taking advantage of new forms of transportation, such as railroads and the Erie Canal. Many of them now worked for wages at factories, where they toiled for long days under the watchful eyes of strict foremen and managers. The gap between rich and poor was getting wider. The independence that came with owning your own farm, or your own shop, was fading into memory.

While many people welcomed these changes, others found them terrifying. Markets brought America into contact with a much wider, unfamiliar world. Money opened doors to this world, but it also closed them to people with empty pockets.

A new kind of power, economic power, entered the scene. Men with money built lavish homes and made decisions that could affect the lives of thousands of workers. To some, they seemed to dominate the government and to lord over the cities and towns springing up all over the young nation.

How could ordinary people hope to achieve their dreams in such a country?

In this society, de Tocqueville saw, the ultimate equalizer was the right to vote. Having a vote meant that your ability to influence the government was no more, or no less, than your neighbor's. It meant that political leaders had to listen to your opinions and take heed of your wants. It meant that your share of political power was exactly the same as that of every other citizen.

Given all this, property requirements were more than a nuisance or a simple financial hurdle. For millions of Americans, the power of money reeked of despotism—the same smell that had driven their parents to fight a war for liberty against Great Britain. Their fathers and grandfathers had fought and died in the Revolution. They themselves had defended the United States against

British invasion during the War of 1812. Their numbers were growing and their collective voice was getting louder: From four million people in 1790, the American population had more than doubled, to ten million, by 1820. It was time, they demanded, for all free men to be counted.

One by one, states began to cave in to the pressure.

Delaware (1792) and Maryland (1802)—both states that allowed slavery—swept away voting property requirements for all free men. Twenty years later, Massachusetts finally dropped its property requirements. During those debates, aging revolutionaries such as the former president John Adams fought tooth and nail to limit the vote to men who owned property, arguing that common men could not be trusted to choose their leaders responsibly. Only the rich, Adams and his allies believed, were smart enough to make decisions. With access to the vote, poor men might use it to check the power of the wealthy elite.

New York (1822) was next, but only after furious debates.

Rich men's fears left them in a bind. How could they oppose voting in a new nation that had trumpeted "no taxation without representation" and that "all men are created equal"? It was a problem that shadowed the ruling class throughout American history—but for the moment, at least, they could not hold back the tide of popular outrage.

EQUALITY?

Every new state admitted into the Union after 1815 followed the principle of "universal manhood suffrage"—which meant different things in different places. Some states, like Massachusetts, allowed *all men* to vote, regardless of how much money or property they had. Others, like Illinois, limited the vote to white men only. Racism played a powerful role in American society at this time, and racial equality in any form was on the agenda of few white people.

The end of property qualifications shook the nation like an earthquake—and established a principle that still exists today. Voting, from that moment onward, became a source of power for fighting back against economic inequality in America.

Having been denied the right to vote for so many years, new voters stampeded into politics. By some estimates, over 80 percent of eligible voters cast ballots in presidential elections during those years (compared with only around 65 percent today).

Their hero was a man named Andrew Jackson—a Tennessean who, ironically, was no believer in human equality. Jackson was an enslaver, a sworn enemy of Native Americans, and a racist. He believed in low taxes and cheap land (much of it taken by force from Native tribes). A hero of the War of 1812 against Great Britain, Jackson had a reputation as a fighter who boasted no formal education; his nickname, Old Hickory, spoke to his common touch at a time when most politicians came from the upper class. He touted himself as the champion of the common (white) man and rode a huge wave of popular support in the early 1820s.

When he ran for president in 1824, Andrew Jackson received more votes than any candidate in American history up to that point. Presidential elections at that time had been quiet affairs; Jackson's was a rowdy celebration of the power of ordinary men who believed that, at last, America had made good on the promises of its Revolution.

Four presidential candidates were on the ballot that year. Jackson was the overwhelming favorite, winning 99 electoral votes out of a total of 261. But the US Constitution required that the winner get a *majority* of electoral votes, or 131—and with the votes split four ways, no candidate could claim that prize. So, according to the rules, the election was thrown to the House of Representatives to decide who would become the next president.

The rules gave each state one vote, and each state delegation (the elected representatives from that state) could vote however they wanted to. In the end, John Quincy Adams, the son of the same former president who publicly opposed giving voting rights to all men, emerged as the victor.

How could this have happened? For the first time, one of the mechanisms specifically designed to hold back the power of the people had done its job.

The framers of the Constitution did not believe in the ability of ordinary people to make responsible political choices. So they created a system in which "electors" appointed by state governments would cast votes for the president and vice president directly, to insulate their decisions from the whims of popular opinion. In the United States, at least in the beginning, voters could not choose the leader of their own country.

Over time, some states changed their own laws so that electors *had* to follow the popular vote, while others kept the old system of giving electors the ability to make their own choice. We've had a patchwork system ever since. Each state's rules were, and still are, different.

Our system for electing the US president *still* makes it possible for someone to win the presidency without winning the majority of the votes—and this has happened twice in the past twenty-five years! Is that a flaw in our democracy? A way of holding back people power? Like Andrew Jackson's supporters in 1824, many critics today would say *yes*.

Newspapers dubbed the election of John Quincy Adams a sham, in what was supposed to be a democratic system of government. The people had spoken, and their voices were ignored. Widely perceived as aloof—hardly a "man of the people"—Adams went on to devote much of his presidency to funding roads, shipping ports, and canals to spur economic development, exactly the kind of market-friendly policies that appeared to support the rich at the expense of working people.

Jackson was furious and famously called the election of Adams "a corrupt bargain," alluding to backroom deals in the House of Representatives that may have swayed the vote in Adams's favor. Instead of giving up, Andrew Jackson doubled down and spent the next four years campaigning for president.

In 1828, the people fought back. In the election that year, the number of voters almost doubled, and Andrew Jackson became president in a landslide victory.

For white men, at least, the era of Andrew Jackson felt like a new celebration of their freedom. And they believed that voting was the purest measure of what it meant to be an American because it put them all on an equal footing.

EQUALITY?

If voting in America felt like a party, however, it wasn't a party everyone was invited to. In the 1830s and 1840s, as more and more white men made a rush for the polls, they locked the doors behind them. Millions of *other* Americans learned the hard way that history sometimes flows in two directions at once. While white men rode on a powerful wave of new voting rights, a riptide carried African Americans farther and farther from the shore.

Andrew Jackson's democracy was democracy for white men—which is another way of saying that it wasn't genuine democracy at all. The United States *still* honors Andrew Jackson—a man who enslaved other human beings and forced thousands of Native Americans from their homes—on the twenty-dollar bill. Is it possible that like many Americans in de Tocqueville's time, we still have our own blind spots about democracy in America?

The African American abolitionist Robert Purvis in 1840.

Chapter Two

TWO STEPS BACK

THOUGH A FREE MAN, ROBERT PURVIS OF PHILADELPHIA understood firsthand the horrors of slavery. He was born in 1810, in Charleston, South Carolina, the son of a free Black woman of African and Jewish descent, and a white British father with a prosperous business as a cotton trader. Charleston was the main hub of America's vicious slave trade. South Carolina was so invested in slavery that it had a majority-enslaved population; few places in the United States seemed so at odds with the ideals of American freedom. For an interracial couple and their fair-skinned son, it was a hostile place.

Purvis's family did not shield him from the realities of his heritage. His grandmother, Dido Badaracka, told him stories of her childhood in Africa and her capture and enslavement. She had known freedom. Walking the streets of his hometown, Robert grew up understanding his country's hypocrisy when it came to Black people.

Charleston's jittery white minority kept a close watch over the state's Black majority, policing the color line with vigilance and violence. This meant that under South Carolina law, Purvis's parents could not marry. As a free person of color, Robert's very existence broke the rules of South Carolina's deeply unequal society.

And so, fearing for their safety, the Purvis family eventually fled north, to the bustling city of Philadelphia, Pennsylvania, with their mixed-race son. Though no paradise for African Americans, Philadelphia had a thriving free Black community. It was a place where someone like Robert Purvis could make a home, and a name, for himself.

In Pennsylvania, a Black man could vote. Robert Purvis could shape the laws that affected his life. It seemed a world away from the oppression of South Carolina.

But with each passing year, the Slave Power—as some Northerners called it—seemed to be creeping closer and closer.

After the American Revolution, Black men in Northern states claimed the rights of free people and asserted themselves as American citizens, voting on equal terms with their white neighbors.

Starting in the late 1820s, however, Black Northerners

began to feel a change in the political weather. The expansion of "universal manhood suffrage," the movement that helped propel Andrew Jackson to power, *should* have meant that all Black men could ride the new democracy wave. Instead, just the opposite happened. All of a sudden, Northern states imposed deliberately racial restrictions on who could vote—eroding the rights of Black people even at a time when white people basked in a new era of expanded freedoms.

To give just one example, by 1826, in New York, only *sixty* Black men—out of an African American population of over twenty thousand—could vote.

One explanation for this bitter turn of events was the outlook of Andrew Jackson himself, who never hid his belief in racial inequality and his support for slavery. Another was the growth of the institution of slavery and, with it, the political power of enslavers who were dead set on crushing the rights of Black people, wherever they might be.

Voting mattered to Black people because it was the last line of defense against the growing power of Southern enslavers and their Northern allies.

To fight back against the Slave Power, Black Americans like Purvis created a new political movement called abolitionism. Abolitionists, both Black and white, believed that slavery and racial oppression could not coexist with genuine American democracy. If all American people did not have the power to forge their own destinies, then how could America be called a free country?

Not surprisingly, enslavers hated abolitionists, and did everything they could to shut down the new democracy movement. Southern authorities intercepted letters coming from the North, checking them for antislavery propaganda. Their agents in Congress passed a "gag rule"—making it impossible for members of the House of Representatives to discuss antislavery proposals. The very *idea* of freedom and equality for Black people terrified the defenders of slavery.

But many white Northerners hated abolitionists as well. Some were simply racists who could never accept racial equality and had no problem with slavery. Others believed that abolitionists were upsetting the delicate balance between the North and South; to them, peace was more important than democracy. Still others thought abolitionism was bad for business because their insurance companies, shoe factories, banks, and textile mills profited from slavery.

It could be life-threatening to be an abolitionist in the 1830s. On October 21, 1835, over a thousand Bostonians, including many of that city's most prominent citizens, attacked the abolitionist William Lloyd Garrison and dragged him through the streets with a noose around his neck. On November 7, 1837, a white mob in Alton, Illinois, murdered a newspaper editor and minister named Elijah Lovejoy for promoting abolitionism.

In the face of such violence, abolitionists refused to give up. They saw themselves correctly as the true American patriots, risking their lives if necessary to force America to live up to its ideals.

Together with William Lloyd Garrison, who survived his attack in Boston, Purvis helped found the American Anti-Slavery Society, an organization that proclaimed "slaveholding is a heinous crime." The American Anti-Slavery Society intended to end slavery in America and to achieve equality for Black people.

But as the nation expanded westward, slavery was growing instead of dying. Enslavers seized control of Alabama, Tennessee, Mississippi, Arkansas, and even Texas, expanding the realm of unfreedom and giving the Slave Power more representation in Congress. Cotton was called the "king" of the American economy, producing wealth not only for enslavers but for Northern businessmen who profited from this money-making crop. If it couldn't be stopped, Purvis believed, slavery could choke off democracy's future.

As slavery expanded, so did the shadow it cast over the whole United States. From 1839 until the beginning of the

Civil War in 1861, *every new state* that joined the United States barred Black people from voting.

For Black people living in the North, the threat of slavery was not abstract. Southern enslavers conspired with patrollers (sometimes called "blackbirds") who stalked the streets of Philadelphia, New York, New Haven, and Boston. These terrifying men seized unsuspecting African Americans (deemed "runaways" even if they had been born free people in the North) and hauled them onto ships bound for the slave states. Many Northern governments allowed this kidnapping to happen openly.

Without political power, African Americans found their very freedom was in jeopardy.

In addition to his abolitionist activism, Purvis was also one of the first "conductors" of the Underground Railroad, a secret network of mostly African Americans who helped enslaved people escape from the South and find new homes in the North and Canada. Conductors like Purvis risked their livelihoods and safety to destroy the system of slavery, person by person.

Free Black Americans like Robert Purvis were challenging the color line and proving that slavery contradicted American freedom. To some, that meant they had to be stopped.

In the summer of 1837, Robert Purvis learned what the opponents of democracy had in mind. Lawmakers in Pennsylvania had been meeting in the state capital of Harrisburg that year to rewrite the state constitution, in part to remove the last property qualifications for voting—a popular move among the growing electorate. Some white leaders in Pennsylvania worried, however, that this would also have the effect of *increasing* the number of Black voters. Their solution was to limit all voting to white men only. And in early 1838, they drafted a new state constitution that proposed just that.

It was now up to Pennsylvania's voters to decide. Robert Purvis believed that he could convince them to cast a vote for democracy.

The veteran people-power advocate put all his powers into a single pamphlet, which he distributed throughout the state.

The Appeal of Forty Thousand Citizens, Threatened with Disfranchisement, to the People of Pennsylvania made the case for democracy in Pennsylvania.

Purvis said it plainly. "When you have taken from an individual his right to vote, you have made the government...a mere despotism," he wrote.

In the end, a dejected Purvis lost the battle to convince citizens of his home state that the right to vote should not be defined by the color of a person's skin—and he lost his right to vote when Pennsylvania voters ratified their state's new, racist constitution on October 9, 1838.

Today, it is technically illegal to stop people from voting because of the color of their skin. But the fight for African American voting rights launched by African Americans in the early nineteenth century lasted for another 150 years and more. The final chapters in this book will show how supposedly race-neutral laws *still in force today* can keep Black people away from the polls. The struggle for color-blind voting rights is alive and well.

The movement for people power was caught in a viselike grip. Words, persuasion, and pamphlets could only call out the problem. But without enough votes—and with political power in the hands of enslavers and their allies—Black Northerners watched as the promises of the Revolution were slowly being choked off.

As Black Northerners' political power decreased, their lives grew more and more precarious.

"We have no protection in law," the Black abolitionist David Ruggles argued, "because the legislators withhold justice."

On July 5, 1852, Frederick Douglass spoke before a

large audience in Rochester, New York, at an Independence Day celebration commemorating the signing of the Declaration of Independence. Douglass was one of the most powerful orators and writers of his time. Born into slavery in Maryland, he escaped as a young man and made his way to freedom—only to discover that for Black Americans freedom everywhere was at risk. Like Robert Purvis, Douglass concluded that his only option was to launch himself into the battle against slavery. For Douglass, the threat of slavery, racism against Black people, and the attack on voting rights were all parts of the same question: How can democracy for all people exist in an unequal nation?

That day, Douglass's words rang out over the crowd, in a speech that would go down as one of the most memorable and influential in all of American history:

> What, to the American slave, is your 4th
> of July? I answer; a day that reveals to
> him, more than all other days in the year,
> the gross injustice and cruelty to which
> he is the constant victim. To him, your
> celebration is a sham.

Frederick Douglass posed a question that America was not yet ready for. It would take a civil war to find the answer.

Robert Smalls in 1870.

Chapter Three

LIBERATION

In the early-morning darkness of May 13, 1862, a young, enslaved man named Robert Smalls waited quietly on the deck of the *Planter*, a Confederate steamboat moored in the harbor at Charleston, South Carolina, not far from the spot where the first shots of the Civil War were fired just over a year earlier. The states of the Confederacy were now in open rebellion against the United States of America, having seceded from the Union in order to protect the institution of slavery. In his own way, Robert Smalls was about to do his part to make sure that they did not succeed.

His plan was, in almost every way, impossible. With the white crew and captain ashore for the night, Smalls and a group of other enslaved people planned to impersonate them and sail boldly out of the harbor, right past Fort Sumter and its cannons, which could sink them in seconds. They planned on delivering the vessel into the hands of a fleet of Union warships blockading Charleston's harbor, ten miles off the coast—if those ships didn't mistake Smalls for an enemy and open fire on him.

To make matters even more complicated, Smalls planned to make a stop on his way out of the harbor to pick up precious cargo: his wife, daughter, infant son, and stepdaughter, all of whom were enslaved as well.

Just before sunrise, Smalls fired the *Planter*'s engines and pulled away from the wharf. He steered the ship carefully through tricky currents, picked up his waiting family, and steamed out of the mouth of Charleston's heavily armed harbor, while Confederate sentries watched him pass.

No one suspected a thing.

Shortly after sunrise, flying the white flag of surrender, Robert Smalls pulled the *Planter* alongside a Union ship and handed it over to the astonished commander. Smalls had done it. He and his family were finally free.

Smalls became a legend for his daring theft—of himself, his family, and a Confederate steamboat.

But Smalls was actually in good company. Many thousands of enslaved Black people "stole" themselves during the Civil War, running away to Union lines and depriving their former enslavers of their labor. One hundred eighty thousand formerly enslaved people joined the Union Army and fought to defeat the Slave Power.

Formerly enslaved people like Robert Smalls knew that ending slavery was just the beginning. Freedom had to mean something more than just not-slavery, more than just the defeat of their former enslavers. Black Americans yearned to live lives outside the control of white people, and to choose for themselves where they could live, how they could make a living, and what kind of government they should live under.

When the Civil War ended, Robert Smalls joined the victorious Union forces in Charleston—where the war had begun—for a victory celebration. People crowded the city by the thousands to watch the American flag raised again. Smalls stood proudly in full uniform on the deck of the *Planter*, which was docked again in the harbor.

Freedom was on everyone's minds. But what would this mean for four million formerly enslaved people? They soon learned that in 1865, after four years of war and many generations of captivity, they had earned (in the words of one witness) "nothing *but* freedom."

Many white Southerners hoped to go back to business as usual. Slavery had been destroyed, but they had other schemes for keeping Black people in servitude. President Andrew Johnson, from Tennessee, made no real move to stop them from doing so.

A set of harsh laws called the Black Codes attempted to return Black Southerners to something as close to slavery as possible. In South Carolina, the Black Codes made it illegal for African Americans to own guns not intended for hunting. It called Black workers "servants" and their employers "masters"—and even required servants to get their masters' permission to leave work. In fact, not working for a white person was called "vagrancy" and was illegal under the Black Codes. Black and white people could not marry each other. And no Black person would ever be permitted to vote.

African American people saw through the new Black Codes immediately. They needed power—the kind of power that would let them not only fight back against the Black Codes but also write their own laws and create their own, more just society.

A month after the end of the war, Frederick Douglass had foreseen that "slavery is not abolished until the black man has the ballot. While the Legislatures of the South retain the right to pass laws making any discrimination between black and white, slavery still lives there."

LIBERATION

For Black people all over the South, the real battle for democracy—for the vote—was only beginning.

In 1866, a new group of Republican congressmen and senators rode to victory in that year's elections. Formed in 1854, the Republican Party opposed the expansion of slavery. In 1861, following the election of the first Republican president, Abraham Lincoln, slaveholding states were prompted to secede from the Union, a move that triggered the Civil War. The Radical Republicans were committed to racial justice, and their success in 1866 reflected Northern voters' outrage over the South's treatment of Black people, and President Johnson's refusal to uphold democracy in the former states of the Confederacy.

These legislators realized that the time had come to put the weight of the federal government behind equal rights for all citizens, Black and white. They had a word for this new plan: *Reconstruction.*

The following spring, they passed the Reconstruction Act of 1867. The act abolished the Black Codes, sweeping away white Southerners' attempts to bring back anything like slavery. More important, perhaps, it called for *all* men in the former states of the Confederacy, Black and white, to be permitted to vote. Each state held a convention to write a new state constitution based on true universal manhood suffrage. And the following year, Black men participated in elections in all parts of the South.

Only a few years earlier, four million enslaved men and women had suffered under the largest slave society in world history. Now they played a central role in crafting what a new society might look like, where African Americans stood alongside white people on equal terms.

This period became known as "Radical Reconstruction," but it might have been called the "Second American Revolution," a term that some people use today.

With the vote, formerly enslaved people sought to transform Southern society. They voted for Black sheriffs who protected, rather than terrorized, their families. They voted for Black mayors who made sure their interests were represented in their local communities, by building badly needed roads and public services. South Carolina, a Black-majority state, voted to create its first public school system. Louisiana went one step further, not only establishing a public school system for all children but voting to make it racially integrated.

All over the South, Black voters put their own representatives in public office—eventually electing over *two thousand* African American men to nearly every political post. From local city councilmen and mayors to state senators, congressmen, lieutenant governors, and even a governor, Black men held positions in nearly every level of government:

- Two US ambassadors
- Two US senators
- Fourteen US representatives
- Forty-three postal officials
- Six hundred eighty-three state representatives
- One hundred twelve state senators
- Six lieutenant governors
- Nine secretaries of state
- One hundred forty-six city council members
- Two hundred thirty-two justices of the peace or magistrates
- Forty-one sheriffs
- Thirty-five tax collectors
- Seventy-nine board of education members

And hundreds of others.

To those who lived through this time, it was almost as if the United States had fast-forwarded hundreds of years in a few short months.

With the vote, African Americans could finally play a role in carving out their own destiny and in protecting their families and their communities. Black people viewed voting as not just another right but as the "heart and soul of their freedom."

Despite the revolution having taken place in the South, however, the Reconstruction Acts did not apply to border states such as Tennessee, West Virginia, or Maryland, which had never joined the Confederacy, despite their support for slavery. And the new laws did not apply to the many Northern states, where Black men were *still* barred from voting.

In short, being able to vote depended on where you lived—a grossly unequal state of affairs. The contrast was not lost on many in Congress.

In 1868, the Republican Party again won the presidential election, sending a Civil War general named Ulysses S. Grant to the White House. Following Grant's inauguration, Congress took up one of the greatest debates in all of American history: whether to amend the US Constitution to establish a national right to vote.

The battle for the Fifteenth Amendment was an epic clash between powerful forces on both sides: those who believed that only the states could decide who should vote and those who believed that the Civil War had settled this issue, in the same way that the American Revolution had settled the question of American independence.

At last, in the spring of 1870, after months of clashes on the floors of the House and Senate, the forces of democracy gained the upper hand.

"The irresistible tendency of modern civilization," Republican senator Samuel Pomeroy explained, "is in the direction of the extension of the right of suffrage.... The day when a few men did the voting and governing for the many has gone by."

THE FIFTEENTH AMENDMENT TO THE UNITED STATES CONSTITUTION

Section 1
The right of citizens of the United States to vote shall not be denied or abridged by the United States or by any State on account of race, color, or previous condition of servitude—

Section 2
The Congress shall have the power to enforce this article by appropriate legislation.

When the Fifteenth Amendment became law, Americans everywhere sensed the impact immediately. President Ulysses S. Grant called it "the most important event that has occurred since the nation came into life."

Black men all over the country—including Robert Purvis of Philadelphia—could finally vote once again.

African American leaders proclaimed the Fifteenth Amendment "a greater revolution than that of 1776." This was not just about the end of slavery but the beginning of something that would give power to Black people all over the country. Many thousands came out to celebrate. Parades jammed the streets of Baltimore, New York, and other cities where African Americans could now vote for the first time in over forty years.

Four years later, Robert Smalls was elected to the US House of Representatives, representing the same district where he had been born into slavery. Smalls traveled to Washington, DC, and claimed his place in the halls of Congress, a place that for most of American history up to that point had been dominated by enslavers.

Robert Smalls joined a new generation of Black leaders, many of them formerly enslaved, swept into public life by a new wave of democracy in America.

A jubilant Frederick Douglass commented, "Never was revolution more complete."

Elizabeth Cady Stanton and her daughter, Harriot. from a daguerreotype 1856.

The women's suffrage pioneer Elizabeth Cady Stanton in 1856.

Chapter Four

SUFFRAGE

THE MESSAGE OF THE FIFTEENTH AMENDMENT TURNED
out to be irresistible.

Some women listened to the debates over the amendment's passage and wondered: Why shouldn't all Americans, men *and* women, have a voice in shaping their own government?

The suffragists, as they were known, were ready to seize their chance. Hundreds of thousands of Americans had died in a war to end slavery. In the aftermath, the government finally stepped in to expand the right to vote beyond white men. The door was ajar; perhaps, they believed, a few brave women could pull it wide open.

These women were ready to cast votes and to choose their own representatives. If not now, when?

The fight for women's suffrage and the quest for racial equality had been intertwined from the very beginning.

While on her honeymoon in England in 1840, a young Elizabeth Cady Stanton attended a historic gathering in London. The World Anti-Slavery Convention was just getting started in the capital of the British Empire. Stanton found a seat in the visitors' gallery. She looked on as politicians, activists, and religious leaders (all men) gave thunderous speeches condemning human bondage. It was a thrilling event for her—and it made her feel that a new society, based on liberty and equality, might actually be on the horizon.

But something unexpected happened when a group of American women arrived in the meeting hall to participate as delegates to the conference. The same men who had moments earlier spoken in favor of equality demanded that these women be ejected from the floor. This was a place for men, they argued, not for women. The proper place for women, in their view, was in the spectators' gallery, where Stanton sat stunned as the scene unfolded.

The troubling memories of the London conference stayed with Stanton when she returned to her home in New York and took up her duties as a wife and mother. As with most white women of her background, her options were limited, and she chafed against them. Still, at that moment in history, she had no idea what she might do to change things. Women simply did not have that power.

Inequality between men and women was a fact of American life, in which women found themselves confined to narrow, sometimes suffocating gender roles. They could manage households but not businesses. They could speak at church but not in a courtroom or on a jury. They could buy things but not own property themselves. Only in very rare cases could they work outside the home, and when they did, it caused a stir. They could cultivate their knowledge of the world but could not attend college. By law and by custom, men ruled over women and made the important decisions that affected their lives.

Of all the things out of reach for women, voting was the furthest. America had become a nation where voting was almost always limited to white men—a so-called democracy where people power was held by a numerical minority of the population that jealously guarded that power.

Women faced a vexing problem. Without the vote—that

is, without the power to change the rules that kept them excluded—how could they ever achieve true equality? Only men voted, and therefore only men wrote the laws. In every state in America, the system itself seemed permanently rigged against them.

Eight years later, Lucretia Mott, one of the American women who had been excluded from participating in the Anti-Slavery Convention in London, passed through Stanton's hometown and called on her for tea (the two had briefly met at that ill-fated event). They were soon joined by other local activists who shared the feeling that the time had come to fight for the rights of women, too.

They put an ad in the local newspaper, announcing a meeting several days later at a Methodist church in Seneca Falls. To their complete astonishment, more than three hundred people, both men and women, showed up.

What later became known as the Seneca Falls Convention felt to the participants like the start of something important. Stanton drafted a declaration calling for women's equality in all aspects of life (that is, everything men took for granted): working, owning property, appearing freely in public, getting a formal education. The members of the convention approved the document and published it as a Declaration of Sentiments, which, powerfully and cleverly, borrowed from the United States' original Declaration of Independence:

> **We hold these truths to be self-evident: that all men and women are created equal; that they are endowed by their Creator with certain inalienable rights; that among these are life, liberty, and the pursuit of happiness; that to secure these rights governments are instituted, deriving their just powers from the consent of the governed.**

To Stanton and her new allies, equality between men and women was a truth that the men who controlled the United States had denied. Women did not have to consent to this unequal situation, Stanton believed. They did not have to sit in the gallery and look on while men made the decisions that governed their lives. But to change things, they first had to take a brave step out into the world, a place where they had few legal rights and no political voice.

Even at Seneca Falls, however, the question of voting rights for women was a hot topic, and the participants agreed to include voting in the convention's resolutions only after hours of heated debate. By this time, most white men had enjoyed the right to vote for several years, but even those attending the meeting did not seem ready to share it.

Inspired by the Seneca Falls meeting, women all over the Northern states organized the first women's rights conventions. In front of overflow crowds in places such as Buffalo, Cleveland, and Albany, they took to the stage and spoke eloquently about gender equality. For the first time in American history, large numbers of women used their voices and their collective strength to force their way into public life.

No Black women attended the convention at Seneca Falls. Americans are *still* taught today that Seneca Falls was the beginning of the women's rights movement in the United States, when in fact Black women had already begun advocating on their own for women's rights several years earlier. Their passion and bravery helped fuse abolitionism and women's rights into a single freedom movement.

Few abolitionists electrified crowds more than Sojourner Truth. Standing six feet tall, and with a clear and commanding voice, Truth condemned slavery from the perspective of her own, painful experience—not as a person enslaved in the South but as someone who had lived the first part of her life enslaved in the North, until she escaped.

Truth spoke with a slight Dutch accent, which she had inherited from her Dutch-speaking parents, both of whom were enslaved by a Dutch man in upstate New York. Sojourner Truth was living proof that slavery hung over the lives of all Black Americans, women and men, no matter where they lived. She showed that for Black women, abolitionism and women's rights could not be disentangled.

The fight to end women's oppression *had* to include the abolition of slavery since so many enslaved people were women.

Together, Black and white women, despite many differences, united into a single force. And when the war against slavery was won, this new generation of women activists, Black and white, had no intention of retreating to the sidelines. After years of campaigning, however, they still lacked the one tool that would grant them real power in America: the vote.

Without the vote, the dream of women's equality would remain just that—a dream.

Reconstruction showed women that it was possible for the government to step in and enforce equal rights. If African Americans in the South could enjoy all the rights and protections of citizens—at least in principle—then why not women everywhere? And if women, Black and white, had played such important roles in the abolition of slavery, then why should they not now claim their "inalienable rights"?

In 1866, suffragists and abolitionists, including Frederick Douglass, Elizabeth Cady Stanton, Susan B. Anthony, and Lucretia Mott, founded the American Equal Rights Association "to secure Equal Rights to all American citizens, especially the right of suffrage, irrespective of race, color or sex." Their plan was to finish the work started by abolitionists and women's rights activists before the Civil War.

In 1869, after the US Congress had passed the Fifteenth Amendment and sent it to the states for ratification, the American Equal Rights Association held a fateful meeting to discuss the issue of women's suffrage. Allies from the abolitionist movement and the campaign for women's rights filled the convention hall.

Should they rally to support the Fifteenth Amendment—which gave Black men, but not women, the right to vote?

On one side of the debate, abolitionists argued that the destruction of slavery, and the real threat of racism in

America, made the passage of the Fifteenth Amendment absolutely necessary. It was a chance, they said, for America to widen the circle of democracy and finish the work of abolitionism to which many of them had devoted their lives.

On the other side, many in the room, including Elizabeth Cady Stanton, wanted to oppose the amendment unless it gave women the right to vote. Stanton argued that rather than a step forward for democracy, the amendment would create an "aristocracy of sex" in America, with women permanently stuck on the lower rung of society. A civil war had been fought to end human bondage—shouldn't the United States follow through and extend the right to vote to women?

Almost 150 years later, in the spring of 2007, echoes of this same debate could be heard inside the Democratic Party primaries, in which voters would choose who should be the party's nominee for president of the United States: Hillary Clinton, a white woman, or Barack Obama, a Black man. Some white feminists argued that it was more important to vote for Clinton, given the need to overcome the long history of sexism. Supporters of Obama (many of them Black women) argued that feminism did not have to be "either/or"—and that it was possible to vote for Obama and still stand proudly as advocates for both gender and racial equality.

In her remarks at the American Equal Rights Association meeting, Elizabeth Cady Stanton poisoned the debate with openly racist opinions. How could America stoop to giving the right to Black men, she insisted, who were not equal to white women such as herself? She referred to Black men by the racist slur "Sambo" and called them "unlettered and unwashed ditch diggers, boot-blacks, butchers and barbers, fresh from the slave plantations of the South."

In addition to sheer racial bigotry, Stanton betrayed her blindness to the challenges of Black men and women in America. White women like Stanton could not seem to understand what Black women could never forget—that women could never gain full equality in America until they defeated racism and racial discrimination.

Even Stanton's longtime allies, many of them African Americans, recoiled at her message. It became clear to them, at that moment, that many of the white women in the women's rights movement were not true allies in the cause of racial equality.

"I must say," Frederick Douglass offered in a passionate speech from the convention stage, "that I do not see how any one can pretend that there is the same urgency in giving the ballot to woman as to the negro. With us, the question is a matter of life and death."

SUFFRAGE

The short-lived American Equal Rights Association collapsed under the weight of disagreement, and its participants went their separate ways.

From that moment on, the movement for women's suffrage broke into two camps, largely divided along racial lines. The split lasted for decades—and the strength that Black and white women had found together deflated like a punctured tire as progress toward women's suffrage ground to a halt.

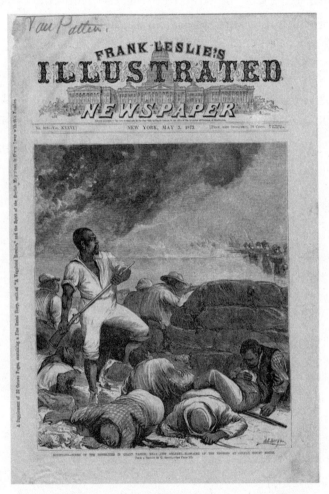

A lithograph showing a scene from the Colfax Massacre, 1872.

Chapter Five

BETRAYAL

BLACK MEN MAY HAVE WON THE VOTE, BUT THE FIFTEENTH Amendment did not mean peace for African Americans.

In cities, towns, and out-of-the-way places, former enslavers and their allies turned to guerrilla warfare, in a yearslong campaign of violence, intimidation, and murder meant to chip away at the new world of people power in the South.

Black Southerners held up their end by defending democracy. Would the federal government keep its own promises?

Some white Southerners didn't wait to find out.

As the sun went down in towns across the South, dark figures appeared on the horizon, accompanied by the pounding of hooves and terrifying shouts. These "night riders" wore white robes, toted torches, and brandished rifles, refusing to show their faces to their victims but making their presence known in a new reign of terror.

Any Black person who asserted the right to vote learned to fear the night riders. Their goal was to terrorize Black communities, making it feel too risky to get involved in politics.

Of the numerous terrorist groups that organized after 1865, the most famous was the Ku Klux Klan, or KKK. The Ku Klux Klan was organized by Colonel Nathan Bedford Forrest of Tennessee, a defeated Confederate who believed that through violence, white Southerners might be able to restore the region to something similar to what existed under slavery.

KKK terrorists had two main targets: any Black person who tried to vote and any white person, especially US Army soldiers, who tried to protect them.

Protecting voting in the South required armed American soldiers. *Keeping* soldiers in the South depended on the commitment of the federal government—backed up by the support of the Northern voting public—to provide them, year in and year out.

Black Southerners had the right to vote for less than three years before they sensed it might be in danger.

In the fall of 1872, President Ulysses S. Grant was reelected president, and Republicans held on to their control of Congress, ensuring, for the time being, that Reconstruction and the government's commitment to voting would continue in the South.

But that same year, a spasm of violence in Louisiana foretold what many white supremacists had in store for democracy and African American voting rights.

Following the election, two candidates for governor of Louisiana claimed victory: a Republican and former US senator named William Pitt Kellogg and his opponent, a former Confederate soldier (and an opponent of Reconstruction) named John McEnery. Terrorism and cheating marred the campaign, and neither side was willing to budge.

By January 1873, two separate governors claimed to be the legitimate leader of Louisiana. All over the state, Republicans who had been fairly elected braced for more violence as rumors circulated that white vigilantes had plans to run them out of the state.

At stake for Black Louisianans that year was not simply a governor's race: Their political survival, and right to vote, was on the line.

In the town of Colfax, several hundred local African Americans and Republican leaders assembled near the courthouse to defend it against rumors of an attack. They dug trenches around it, gathered their few weapons, and took shelter inside.

For three weeks, the defenders held their ground. But on Easter Sunday 1873, a large group of white militiamen, including former Confederate soldiers and Ku Klux Klansmen, forced their way into Colfax. The heavily armed troop even rolled a cannon into town.

The boom of the cannon announced the attack. For over two hours, huddled in their trenches, the courthouse defenders held off the white supremacist force with rifle fire and pistol shots. But their smaller numbers and exposed position were no match for their enemies.

Surrounded on all sides, they surrendered to the white militia at nightfall. But that was when the real violence started. After the small number of white Republicans left the courthouse, the militiamen opened fire on the building, killing dozens of Black men who tried to surrender.

Later that night, under the cover of darkness, the attackers lined up and executed as many as fifty African Americans, then dumped their bodies in the Red River. They showed no mercy for Black people who were defending their rights. The murders were intended as a warning: Voting, for African Americans, could mean a death sentence.

White Southerners commemorated the event as the Colfax Riot. For the next 150 years (until 2021), a historical marker at the site described it as "the end of carpetbag

[Northern] misrule in the South," downplaying both the massacre and its role in crushing democracy. The victors wrote a whitewashed version of the story. For generations, textbooks, novels, and even movies (such as the 1915 silent film *Birth of a Nation*, which was the first movie ever shown in the White House) depicted Reconstruction as a time when Black people and their white allies ruled the South through corruption and violence.

Black Louisianans, however, remembered the truth, and had their own term for what happened that night in 1873: the Colfax Massacre.

For the next four years, white attacks on Black voters grew more and more determined, and violent. Black Southerners did everything they could to strengthen democratic institutions in the states of the former Confederacy. They kept on voting, running for office, and exercising their constitutional rights.

Having survived captivity, they knew, more than anyone, what was at stake if they didn't succeed.

By 1876, democracy itself was on the ballot in the South, as both parties geared up for an election fight that would determine the future of Reconstruction.

During the election that fall, white South Carolinians

opposed to Reconstruction created an armed militia called the Red Shirts, a group with a clearly stated battle plan to make it impossible for Black people—and Republicans more generally—to cast a vote in South Carolina.

A copy of their plan circulated all over the state:

> Every Democrat must feel honor bound to control the vote of at least one Negro.... Never threaten a man individually. If he deserves to be threatened, the necessities of the times require that he should die. A dead Radical is very harmless—a threatened Radical...is often troublesome, sometimes dangerous, and always vindictive.

Even though this plan was illegal, and called for overthrowing a democratically elected government through violent attacks, and even murder, the Red Shirts were not shy about promoting it openly. In fact, Red Shirt militia groups accompanied the Democratic candidate for governor, Wade Hampton III, as he toured the state that fall. Hampton was a former enslaver and Confederate general who aimed to "redeem" the state from Republican rule.

The violent tactics seemed to work. As many as 150 people died on Election Day, as Red Shirts and white "rifle clubs" fought to keep Black voters from the polls and filled the ballot boxes with fake votes for Hampton.

A white South Carolinian named Ben Tillman later bragged in racist terms on the floor of the US Senate about his role in the overthrow of democracy in the fall of 1876:

> Then it was that we stuffed ballot boxes, because desperate diseases require desperate remedies, and having resolved to take the State away, we hesitated at nothing....Eighteen hundred and seventy-six happened to be the hundredth anniversary of the Declaration of Independence, and the action of the white men of South Carolina in taking the State away from the negroes we regard as a second declaration of independence by the Caucasian from African barbarism.

(Tillman served two terms as governor of South Carolina, from 1890 to 1894, and was a US senator from 1895 to 1918.)

White South Carolinians honored Wade Hampton's "victory" by erecting statues of him and naming towns, schools, and even golf courses in his honor. You can see many of Wade Hampton's memorials and plaques around the state to this day. They silently commemorate a time when Black people's votes were stolen from them.

Black Americans already had good reason to doubt the commitment of their white allies to equal voting rights. But with dark clouds on the horizon, even they did not anticipate the destructive power of the political storm coming their way.

The attacks against Black Republicans in the South tipped the 1876 presidential election campaign into near chaos, with neither the Republican Rutherford B. Hayes nor the Democrat Samuel Tilden emerging as the clear winner. As Electoral College votes were tallied, *both* Democrats and Republicans claimed victory in three states marred by racial violence: South Carolina, Louisiana, and Florida.

Weeks of secret negotiations among congressional leaders and Democratic and Republican party officials resulted in what became known as the Compromise of 1877, by which the Democratic Party agreed to accept the Republican Hayes's victory—as long as the federal government agreed to withdraw its troops (the same ones protecting Black voters) from the South.

By the spring of 1877, the Second American Revolution sputtered to a halt. Many white politicians, it seemed, were willing to abandon the same Black voters who had supported them for nearly a decade, in exchange for holding on to their own political power.

Left to fend for themselves, however, Black Southerners bravely continued to vote, whenever and wherever they could.

Robert Smalls refused to abandon his quest for equal rights and political power. A savvy politician and businessman, he managed to purchase his former enslaver's house in Beaufort, South Carolina—the same place where he was born and worked as a child alongside his mother for the McKee family.

With the support of his local African American constituents, Smalls won reelection to Congress four times, holding his seat until 1887. He was one of the few Black legislators to survive the onslaught of violence against the African American community in his home state. During these perilous years, he did as much with his political power as he could to benefit his local community, starting a school, opening a newspaper, and attracting government funds to rebuild the city's port.

Smalls was the exception, however. Of the more than two thousand democratically elected Black officeholders, few survived the violence that brought Reconstruction to an end. White vigilantes forced many of them out of office and made sure that no Black person dared to run again.

The white South managed to keep most Black people from voting, or running for office, for the next *ninety* years.

After Reconstruction, no Black person became governor of a Southern state—or any American state—until Douglas Wilder was elected governor of Virginia in 1990. Mississippi has *still* not elected an African American senator since Hiram Revels held that post during Reconstruction. In many places, the results of Reconstruction's defeat still linger today.

Some democracy activists, in fact, are now calling for a new Reconstruction to complete the unfinished business of what was begun in 1867. Creating a better, more equal society, they argue, begins with our government stepping in and enforcing voting rights in the strongest possible way.

Meanwhile, the history of Reconstruction was written by the same people who had plotted its downfall. For generations, and in some classrooms today, Americans have been taught that Reconstruction was a failure because

Black Southerners were not ready for democracy and could not handle the responsibilities of government.

But the real story is just the opposite: After the Civil War, African Americans helped create the closest thing to democracy America had ever seen.

Their dream never died.

A receipt for a poll tax payment in Knoxville, Tennessee, 1894.

Chapter Six

DOWNFALL

By the hundredth birthday of the US Constitution, the American people's efforts to create a real democracy had reached a near standstill. Although the nation's population was growing by leaps and bounds, the size of its electorate (people who could legally vote) was shrinking under the pressure of mob violence and discriminatory laws.

Still, people clamored for representation—from rural towns in Mississippi to Asian immigrant neighborhoods in San Francisco and to the overflowing cities of Chicago, New York, and Boston. The United States of America would become either democracy's deathbed or the place where it was reborn.

At that moment, the South, home to the Second American Revolution, had the answer.

Since the overthrow of Reconstruction, Democrats had won elections by stuffing ballot boxes, rigging the voter registration system, and threatening Black voters with physical violence. That they had to do all these things was a testament to just how hard Black people tried to keep voting, even after the federal government abandoned them in 1877.

By the end of the nineteenth century, however, many white politicians grew weary of these unofficial, piecemeal efforts. The time had come, they decided, to rewrite the laws themselves to keep down the Black vote. Beginning with Mississippi in 1890, Southern states held conventions to rewrite their state constitutions, aiming to stop Black men from voting for good.

This was by no means a secret plan; on the contrary, white politicians and newspapers publicly announced their intention to solve the problem of "negro suffrage" once and for all. White supremacists controlled nearly every business, courthouse, and statehouse in the South—and the federal government showed no intention of stopping them.

It was open season for the opponents of people power in the South.

As politicians gathered across the region, racism echoed from the floors of their conventions. When Alabama Democrats gathered in 1900 to set the party platform, the convention chairman proclaimed that "the great question of the Elective Franchise must be settled. The white line was formed in 1874 and swept the white men of Alabama into power. The white line has been re-formed in 1900 to keep them in power forever."

"Discrimination! Why, that is precisely what we propose," declared a Democratic delegate at Virginia's constitutional convention. "That, exactly, is what this Convention was elected for—to discriminate to the very extremity of permissible action under the limitations of the Federal Constitution, with a view to the elimination of every negro voter who can be gotten rid of, legally, without materially impairing the numerical strength of the white electorate."

The Democratic Party leadership of North Carolina published this statement in the Raleigh *News and Observer* in November 1898: "North Carolina is a WHITE MAN's state and WHITE MEN will rule it."

The South Carolina Constitutional Convention met in 1895 and came up with an openly racist scheme to stop Black men from voting. Robert Smalls of Beaufort, one of the few Black delegates to the convention, refused to sign it.

State by state, Southern politicians came up with an ingenious three-part plan to lock in white supremacy.

Part one was to charge voters money to cast a ballot in an election. These poll taxes were designed to limit the number of Black people who could vote.

Beginning in 1904, for example, every voter in Virginia had to pay a poll tax of $1.50 for each of the three years prior to the next election, for a total of $4.50. The amounts may seem small, but they are the equivalent of $150 in 2023—enough to keep millions of Americans away from the polls. (Most African Americans in the South worked on land owned by white people and had little or no access to cash.)

Part two was putting in place literacy and other tests, which all voters had to pass before they could register to vote.

Would-be voters had to show up at a county courthouse and take a written test, administered by a white registrar or court official. These same officials decided who passed—and who didn't. They made certain that Black applicants rarely, if ever, succeeded in passing the test.

The questions were intentionally designed to stump the test takers. Tests like these were administered across the South until the 1960s.

Here is one from Alabama:

Question: Does enumeration affect the income tax levied on citizens in various states?

Answer: Yes

And another from Georgia:

Question: How does the Constitution of Georgia provide that a county site may be changed?

Answer: By a two-thirds vote of the qualified voters of the county, voting at an election held for that purpose and by a majority of the vote of the General Assembly. (Article XI, Section I, Paragraph IX of the Georgia State Constitution. Code Section 2-7809.)

Officials could decide on the spot if an answer wasn't sufficient (even if it was entirely correct) or if a would-be voter's command of grammar was faulty.

At a time when most Southerners lacked formal education, and many were completely illiterate, the tests formed a river that could not be crossed.

Poll taxes and literacy tests proved very effective at stopping Black people from voting.

They had little or no cash to begin with, thanks to their stingy white employers. Many, too, had no formal schooling, thanks to the Southern states' meager investment in education. For most, *not* voting was the only possible option.

However, it turned out that poll taxes and literacy tests *also* prevented many white people—like their Black neighbors, impoverished and poorly educated—from voting as well. To get around the new restrictions, and to keep white voters from getting angry at them, the South's political leaders worked out a solution.

"Grandfather clauses" were laws that allowed men to vote if their grandfathers had voted or served in the Confederate Army or if they themselves had registered to vote before 1867. The clauses were a kind of safety valve for the many white voters who could not pay poll taxes or pass literacy tests; it allowed them to vote anyway. Nearly all Black voters' grandparents had been enslaved, and as such could not vote—and no Black person had been allowed to register before 1867.

The Supreme Court declared grandfather clauses

unconstitutional in 1915—a decision that in no way deterred Southern politicians. In response to the court's decision, Oklahoma declared that anyone not registered to vote—that is, mostly Black men—had to register between April 30 and May 11, 1916, or lose their right to vote forever. Few succeeded in registering during that impossibly small, twelve-day window.

The Southern plan worked.

In 1896, 130,334 African Americans were on the voter rolls in Louisiana; eight years later that number had dropped to 1,342.

In Mississippi, a state with a Black majority, only 8,615 African American men were registered to vote by 1892.

By 1910, only 4 percent of Black men in Georgia could vote.

Across the South overall, less than 10 percent of eligible Black voters could break through the new wall of white supremacy to cast a ballot.

Thirty years after Reconstruction had brought democracy to the South, racism swept it completely aside. This new, antidemocratic system would stay in place for almost seventy years. Millions of Americans *still alive today* were born, and grew up, under its harsh voting restrictions.

Almost immediately, Black people suffered the results of losing the right to vote. It was no accident that the new voting restrictions went hand in hand with the rise of what became known as Jim Crow: a new set of laws that forced African Americans into a separate, second-class existence.

White-controlled governments enforced racial segregation in streetcars, in trains, in public libraries, even at water fountains. Black children could attend only separate, poorly funded schools. A Black person accused of a crime always faced an all-white jury. White judges, sheriffs, and police officers laid down the law. And Black workers found themselves shunted into the most grueling, lowest-paid jobs.

Without the vote, African Americans lost their collective power to create a society that protected their rights.

But Black people did not forget what they had accomplished after the Civil War. Those memories would carry the fight forward through the dark times to come.

The South didn't act alone. Anti–people power forces all over the country were on the march in the final years of the nineteenth century.

In the North and West, their targets were not African Americans but rather the millions of new immigrants arriving from Europe and Asia. Fearing the "foreign" influence of Chinese, Japanese, Russian, Polish, Italian, and Puerto Rican immigrants (among many others), the opponents of voting in these places sharpened their own set of tools to prune back the size of the electorate. "Reformers" in the nation's big cities fought successfully for new laws to make it difficult for anyone but native-born citizens to vote.

- Immigrants had long been allowed to vote in many states, even when they weren't citizens. In the 1890s, however, one state after another rolled back their support for what was known as "alien suffrage"; Arkansas was the last state to allow noncitizen voting, until 1926.

- States with large numbers of immigrants, like New York, made literacy tests standard practice—preventing anyone without command of the English language from registering to vote.

- Some states, such as Massachusetts, sought to expand the enforcement of "pauper laws," which banned anyone who received public assistance from voting. Other states passed "taxpayer laws," which limited voting to people who owned real estate or other property in their district. In both cases, the goal was the same: to keep political power in the hands of moneyed, native-born white Americans.

By the end of the nineteenth century, old prejudices found fertile soil and sprouted again. Everywhere, the victories of people-power activists were quietly unraveled in a sustained assault on voting rights.

Part Two

AWAKENING

THE WINTER OF 1899 IN THE UNITED STATES WAS the coldest in recorded history. From the Gulf Coast of Mississippi to the forests of Maine, arctic temperatures plunged the nation into a deep, bone-chilling freeze.

That same year, American democracy seemed to be tracking the weather.

Millions of Americans found chilly receptions at voting booths. Poor people, Black and white, got the cold shoulder when they tried to register—because of either steep poll taxes or daunting literacy tests. New citizenship rules froze out Chinese immigrants and most Native Americans altogether.

At the dawn of a new century, it seemed, only white men basked in the warmth of citizenship. Had they succeeded, finally, in putting people power on ice?

On the sidelines, one group of Americans kept the spark lit for democracy. Some of their grandmothers—or great-grandmothers—had voted before or had fought the longest battle in American history for the right to participate in elections. They gathered their courage. It was time, they argued, for the other half of the United States population to step into the circle and have their voices represented.

To the 8,000,000 Working Women in the United States

Are you satisfied with your working conditions?
Are you satisfied with your living conditions?

What Is Wrong?

You want better food, better homes, better clothes.
You want shorter hours, bigger pay, safe and sanitary workshops.

How Can You Get What You Want?

By UNITING, in the industries, to force the bosses to better your conditions.
    You can do this now.
By UNITING, as women, to secure laws that will protect you.
    You cannot do this now, because

YOU HAVE NO VOTE

All working people should have every possible weapon to enable them to control the conditions under which they must live and work.
Men have one weapon that women lack. They have the vote.
Women should have every weapon that men have, but men deny them the vote.
Is this right?

DEMAND VOTES FOR WOMEN!

MAKE WORKING MEN DEMAND VOTES FOR WORKING WOMEN!

National American Woman Suffrage Association poster, circa 1915.

Chapter Seven

THE FLAME

AMERICAN SUFFRAGISTS HAD KEPT THEIR CAUSE ALIVE
for decades against determined opposition. Finally, in
the early years of the twentieth century, the movement
for women's right to vote gained steam. Suffragists drew
renewed strength and inspiration from their allies overseas, especially in Great Britain, where voting-rights activists had taken their campaign to the next level, in stormy
demonstrations that sometimes verged on violence. (Alice
Paul, an American suffragist who spent time in London,
was arrested along with the suffragist Amelia Brown for
interrupting a speech by the mayor; Brown caused a scene
by shattering a stained-glass window with her shoe.) British suffragists were not content to wait patiently, and they
set an example for their American sisters.

Women around the world began to feel that their time
had come—that voting for women might well happen in

their lifetime. And why not? History had tilted into a new century. Cities were bustling with exciting new inventions and technologies and were bursting at the seams with new arrivals. Society was changing quickly. Wasn't it about time for American democracy to catch up?

On May 4, 1912, in America's largest city, women's suffrage activists decided to show the rest of New York that they were a force to be reckoned with.

That afternoon, women began to line up for what would become one of the largest suffrage parades in American history. They arrived by the thousands, many sporting the three-cornered hats worn by men during the American Revolution—a reference to what the original revolutionaries had *failed* to accomplish when they denied women the vote.

The sheer variety of participants on this day seemed to suggest that the painful divisions of the past had been overcome—or at least had been set aside. Promptly at 5:00 PM, women of many backgrounds and ethnicities proceeded uptown, joined by immigrants, African Americans, and even hundreds of male supporters. The movement surged forward like a river that could not be dammed.

But at the head of the parade, on horseback, was a truly unusual sight: a young woman who was not even old enough to vote. In fact, as a Chinese-born immigrant, she couldn't become an American citizen because of a discriminatory law that had been passed by Congress thirty years earlier.

Mabel Ping-Hua Lee, the teenaged daughter of a Baptist minister, held her gaze steady, smiling at the boisterous crowd. She was surrounded by supporters of voting rights for women, as well as throngs of young men who hurled insults at the marchers and at Mabel herself.

Mabel was a star student at Erasmus Hall High School in Brooklyn (the only Chinese student there), with plans to enter prestigious Barnard College. While she was still a young girl, Mabel began to read about a new democracy movement, not in the United States, but in the country of her birth. She was born in Guangzhou, China, and immigrated with her parents to the United States.

As she grew older, she paid close attention to political upheavals in China, where a new political leader named Sun Yat-sen was fighting to lead a movement for democracy and to overthrow the Qing dynasty. Sun Yat-sen had spent many years in the United States and believed in government "of the people, by the people, and for the people." But he believed that America was flawed because of the way it discriminated against people of color and excluded women from voting.

Young Mabel wouldn't be able to vote as an adult not only because she was a woman, but also because she was a Chinese immigrant and a victim of a long history of anti-Chinese laws and discrimination. White suffragists placed her at the head of their parade, but Mabel understood that her path to equality and political power would be much different from theirs.

Thirty-five years had passed since the suffragists had split over voting rights for Black men. Now, in a new century, a much more diverse movement was pushing its way onto the scene. Some were immigrants, others women of color, still others working women of many different backgrounds. All of them saw voting as the key to improving their lives.

Mabel showed other suffragists that the fight to vote wasn't happening just in America and Europe. Chinese women, in fact, were sprinting ahead of other movements around the world. She believed America could learn something from China.

American suffragists realized that women in China might actually win the vote before they did. The example of the Chinese sparked indignation among American women. How could the world's oldest so-called democracy be lagging so far behind?

At the suffrage parade in New York City, Anna Howard Shaw, head of the National American Woman Suffrage Association, purposely marched behind the Chinatown cohort with a banner that read, "NAWSA Catching Up with China." And just before the Democratic National Convention in Baltimore that summer, she repeated her message: "If the Democratic party wants to catch up with China, they can give women the vote. China has waked up. Will they?"

The message of white suffragists was tinged with anti-Chinese racism. Mabel, however, was proud of her Chinese heritage and critical of how America treated its Chinese population.

"All women are recognized in New York, excepting Chinese women," she said. "She is not included in your educational institutions. Your social and recreational centers do not include her. How can she learn! How can you have half of your people in utter darkness, and the other half in light!"

Chinese people had been coming to America for well over half a century, joining the waves of other migrants from around the world. Employers welcomed their labor, as long as they didn't complain about the working conditions. In fact, some railroad and mining companies, where thousands of Chinese men toiled under dangerous conditions, preferred Chinese employees because it was more difficult for noncitizens to fight back. Because Chinese immigrants could not vote, there was no one to represent their interests.

Some politicians in the western states had opposed the Fifteenth Amendment because they did not want to grant the vote to Chinese men. Like the former enslavers in the South, who wanted to keep the vote out of the hands of Black people, western leaders believed that giving Chinese immigrants the vote would give them power—power to improve their lives and working conditions, and to gain independence from their employers.

At a time when millions of European immigrants claimed their piece of the American dream, the Chinese were treated as an inferior, alien people.

In 1882, this wave of racist feeling resulted in Congress's passing the Chinese Exclusion Act, the first law in American history to ban a specific group of immigrants and the first to restrict immigration in a broad way. The act prevented Chinese workers from immigrating to the United States and also made it impossible for Chinese immigrants to become citizens—which also meant that they could not vote.

With no legal power to defend themselves, Chinese Americans faced harassment, violent attacks, and even forced deportation to China by local authorities. For a time, it seemed as if *anyone* of Chinese descent had no future in the United States.

Chinese Americans, however, refused the idea that they deserved fewer rights than other Americans.

Tye Leung had been a freedom fighter ever since she was a girl, and she knew what it was like to have no power as a woman. When she was only thirteen, her impoverished parents sold her to a man to be his wife. When she was finally rescued from captivity, she vowed never to lose her independence and to help other women gain theirs.

A Chinese woman born in the United States, Tye Leung possessed the rare skill of being able to speak two languages fluently. While still a teen, she helped other young Chinese women escape from slavery and forced labor in San Francisco by translating for them in local courtrooms.

Tye Leung used her language skills to become the first Chinese American woman to be hired by the US government. She worked as an interpreter on Angel Island in San Francisco Bay, helping Chinese immigrants who arrived from overseas but were prevented from entering the country because of laws banning them. Each day, Tye Leung listened to their stories and, bit by bit, gathered news from China and of a democracy movement many thousands of miles away.

"Always, sitting there listening to my countrymen," she said, "I listen for little scraps about the great new movement over the sea, that is setting them free over there as I have been set free here."

When she decided to marry a white man named Charles Schulze, however, Tye Leung was reminded of the limits of American freedom for a woman of color. First, the couple had to travel to Washington State for their marriage ceremony because the state of California outlawed interracial marriages. Next, when they returned, Tye Leung was abruptly fired from her job on Angel Island—not because she had done anything wrong, but because the federal government refused to employ married women.

Tye Leung had a keen sense of the racial and gender barriers holding her back. So, in 1911, when California joined several other western states in allowing women to vote (eight years before women gained that right nationally), Tye Leung seized her chance.

In May 1912, she lined up at a polling place in San Francisco and voted in the presidential primary election—the first Chinese American woman to cast a ballot in the United States. (Because she had been born in the United States, Tye Leung—unlike Mabel Ping-Hua Lee and thousands of other Chinese-born immigrants—was not affected by the Chinese Exclusion Act.)

By some accounts, Tye Leung was the first Chinese woman *anywhere* in the world to vote.

She took this responsibility, and the example she set for others, very seriously.

"My first vote?" she later recalled. "Oh, yes, I thought long over that. I studied; I read about all your men who wished to be president. I learned about the new laws. I wanted to KNOW what was right, not to act blindly." That fall, women like Tye Leung learned how much their votes mattered: The presidential election was the closest in California's history, with Theodore Roosevelt winning the state by only 174 votes. Nationwide, the progressive Roosevelt was not so lucky, and the presidency went to Woodrow Wilson, an ardent supporter of states' rights and white supremacy.

Some newspapers in California pointed to Tye Leung's vote as an argument for why *all* women were ready to participate in electoral politics. For Tye Leung, her vote told a story of what American democracy might look like someday.

In the years following the New York suffrage parade, women of varied nationalities streamed into the suffrage movement. All sought the vote, but they often did so with very different goals in mind.

For wealthy white women, getting the vote meant entering fully into public life. They were fighting to be treated as equals by society and to bring an end to laws that prevented them from controlling their own careers and their own destinies.

Black women saw the vote as a tool not only for achieving equality as women but for the broader fight against Jim Crow. They could never attain true equality, they understood, without also stopping segregation, lynching, and racial discrimination.

Mabel Ping-Hua Lee, Tye Leung, and hundreds of thousands of immigrant women saw voting as the path to belonging and to giving their people a weapon to fight against discrimination.

For working women of many ethnicities and nationalities, the suffrage movement was part of the bigger fight to improve their wages and working conditions. Millions of them were joining the workforce as domestic servants and factory workers—but they were always paid less than men and often suffered sexual harassment and discrimination on the job. Getting the vote might give them the power they needed to change their lives for the better.

That same year, suffrage activists fanned out across Connecticut, distributing leaflets and other materials encouraging women to join the movement. Inspired by them, a young factory worker used her finger to write "Votes for Women" across a filthy window in the building where she toiled for long, dark hours each day. Her male supervisors quickly found and erased it.

By the next morning, the factory managers had scrubbed all the windows, allowing light to stream in for the first time in the young worker's memory.

"Well, if the mere mention of votes for women has that effect," the young woman remarked, "I wonder what the vote itself would do?"

Like millions of women in 1912, she was determined to find out.

Portrait of Zitkála-Šá in 1898.

Chapter Eight

THE STORYTELLER

WHILE WOMEN FROM EVERY CORNER OF THE UNITED
States stoked the suffrage fire in the early twentieth century, a different group of people could only watch from a
distance. They were here first, but their voices were the
last to echo through the halls of power.

Native people had once lived freely, controlling millions of square miles of land. By the end of the nineteenth
century, however, the US government had penned their
communities inside more than two hundred reservations,
all the way from Maine to California. Government agents
spoke for them as their representatives—but not as people
who had their best interests in mind.

The government's plan was for Native Americans to disappear. But a young girl in Montana saw a different future
and a different path: one that led right to the nation's capital.

Zitkála-Šá (meaning "Red Bird") was eight years old

when the white missionaries came to visit her at her home on the Yankton Sioux reservation in South Dakota, where she lived with her mother and several hundred other members of the people of the Seven Council Fires. Her people had once spanned the Great Plains of North America. Now they inhabited only small parcels of land, watched over by government agents and soldiers.

Zitkála-Šá had grown up in the twilight of her people's power. In 1876, the year of her birth, Lakota, Cheyenne, and Arapaho warriors defeated General George Custer's forces at the Battle of Little Bighorn in Montana. Custer's mission had been to conquer the American West with military might, but it ended with humiliation for the general and his men.

The Native warriors' victory, however, was merely a pause in a much longer descent. Their loss of land and power quickened in the final years of the nineteenth century, and Zitkála-Šá saw the world she once knew wither away.

In 1887, Congress passed the Dawes Act, which forced Native American tribes to give up control of their vast lands in exchange for meager 160-acre farming plots. Before the act, Native Americans controlled 150 million acres of land in the western United States; only a few years later, most of this land had been parceled out to white farmers. Native people who refused to comply were herded onto reservations against their will. From then on, every part of their lives, from food to school to housing, was controlled by the US government.

Torn from their lands, many Native Americans became dependent, forced to rely on the same government that had destroyed their way of life. Their survival hung by a thread.

The reservation where Zitkála-Šá lived wasn't a fun place for a child. Her spirits lifted when the missionaries told her about a boarding school they could take her to, filled with Native children like herself. They even promised her all the red apples she could want, a rare snack on the reservation, if she attended school.

What she didn't know was that the boarding school was set up by the government not to educate her but to erase her culture. Schools like this were part of a plan to "assimilate" Native American children—to separate them from their parents and their traditions and to force them to adopt the language and culture of white America. The government argued that boarding schools were a step on the path toward citizenship; they would accomplish this not by educating children but by crushing their cultures.

The name of Zitkála-Šá's school, White's Manual Labor Institute, revealed its purpose, which was to reduce

Native children to obedient workers. Native children were beaten, stripped of their traditional clothing, and forbidden to speak their own languages. By some estimates, more than five hundred children died at these boarding schools.

In the last decades of the nineteenth century, the government took over twenty thousand children from their parents and put them in boarding schools; by 1920, this number had tripled.

After years spent in government schools, Zitkála-Šá took away a different lesson from the one her teachers had intended. To hold on to her people's power, she believed, she had to cling to her identity and her culture, not give it up.

But Zitkála-Šá also understood the painful reality of Native Americans' predicament at the time. Bit by bit, they might reclaim their traditions and identities. But without political power, it was still the US government—through the Bureau of Indian Affairs—that called the shots.

The Bureau of Indian Affairs controlled Native land, education, jobs, health, and housing. Rather than making sure that Native communities had enough, it helped keep them mired in poverty and powerlessness.

With no other tools at her disposal, Zitkála-Šá began to write. She put Dakota stories down on the page to keep them from becoming lost or forgotten. She put new songs to traditional music. She jotted down memories of her experiences with her family, her people—and at the hands of white teachers.

Her writing became a kind of activism, a way of defending her people from the government's attempt to erase them.

In her twenties, Zitkála-Šá achieved fame as a writer and musician. She performed all over the United States and published her writing in the nation's leading magazines, including the *Atlantic* and the *New Republic*. She even published a book, *Old Indian Legends*, to preserve her cultural legacy through the written word.

Whenever she could, she also recorded the history of how the United States tried to take her people's power from them so that no one would forget.

In one of her stories, Zitkála-Šá recounted the day that white staff members at her school forcibly cut off their students' hair. In Lakota culture, short, or "shingled," hair was a sign of weakness—a symbol of someone who had been captured by an enemy. When it became clear to her what was happening, she ran and hid under a bed, in a last-ditch effort to cling to what remained of her family and her power.

> What caused them to stoop and look under the bed I do not know. I remember being dragged out, though I resisted by kicking and

scratching wildly. In spite of myself, I was
carried downstairs and tied fast in a chair.

I cried aloud, shaking my head all the while
until I felt the cold blades of the scissors
against my neck, and heard them gnaw
off one of my thick braids. Then I lost my
spirit. Since the day I was taken from my
mother I had suffered extreme indignities.
People had stared at me. I had been tossed
about in the air like a wooden puppet.
And now my long hair was shingled like a
coward's! In my anguish I moaned for my
mother, but no one came to comfort me.
Not a soul reasoned quietly with me, as
my own mother used to do; for now I was
only one of many little animals driven by a
herder.

Zitkála-Šá's writing attracted the attention of a new
movement for Native American rights that was dawning
at the beginning of the twentieth century. This movement included thousands of people desperate to keep their
Native identities alive, even in the face of defeat. By her
example, Zitkála-Šá showed them that this was possible.

In her quest for power for her people, Zitkála-Šá moved to Washington, DC, and joined the broader movement for women's suffrage. She believed that she could find allies among women who had also experienced the pain of exclusion and the frustration of lacking representation. She added her strong and persuasive voice to the chorus of women calling for the right to vote.

The white leaders of the suffrage movement showed a special interest in her and other Native women who stepped forward to advocate for their rights. A new generation of suffrage activists had studied their history and become familiar with the story of the Haudenosaunee (Iroquois) tradition of government. They were keen to learn about how Haudenosaunee women could own property and played a role in electing their leadership. They believed that Native traditions might show white audiences what was lacking in their own society, even though many looked down on Native peoples. They invited Zitkála-Šá to speak about her own traditions and to talk to audiences about the power of women in her Native community.

It gradually became clear to Zitkála-Šá that her white allies were mainly interested in the past, and not the present issues facing Native women. They encouraged her to

wear traditional clothing and jewelry, but not to reveal
the truth about how their own government was harming
Native people.

Like many other Native American activists, Zitkála-Šá
watched with horror as that truth unfolded in Oklahoma,
when the territory was admitted to the Union as an American state. Oklahoma had been home to hundreds of thousands of Native people, many of them the descendants of
the Cherokee, Chickasaw, Choctaw, Creek, and Seminole
who had survived the Trail of Tears during the presidency
of Andrew Jackson. After Oklahoma became a state in
1907, the courts started declaring "all persons of one-half
or more Indian ancestry to be incompetent to manage their
own affairs" and empowered white "guardians" to make
decisions about the millions of acres of tribal lands. With
no vote, and no political rights, Native people in the state
saw their precious lands plundered by white businessmen.
Zitkála-Šá called it "legalized robbery."

The solution, as she saw it, was for her people to represent themselves. The United States had defeated the
Lakota and other Native tribes on the battlefield, but the
Bureau of Indian Affairs had not succeeded in destroying their memories or their traditions. Native people's best
hope was to speak on their own behalf, on their own terms.
They had as much a claim to exist, freely, as anyone else.

In 1914, Zitkála-Šá joined the recently established Society of American Indians, the first organization in the United States created by and for Native Americans and dedicated to protecting their rights and cultures. The society modeled itself on the National Association for the Advancement of Colored People, or NAACP, which had been founded in 1909. The society realized that political power was the key to defending Native people, that the vote was the key to political power, and that organizing was the key to getting the vote.

She soon became one of its most visible and outspoken activists.

For her, nurturing Native traditions and fighting for voting rights were two sides of the same coin. Native people were threatened with extinction because in the space of a mere twenty years, they had lost the final military battles to protect their communities. At the mercy of the American government, they found themselves persecuted, abused, and disrespected.

Native people needed a new form of power. All around her, Zitkála-Šá saw other Americans claiming their rights as citizens of the same land where she and her people were born. As she saw it, there was only one path forward for her people. And—still a young woman—she would lead the fight for it.

The Silent Sentinels picket the White House in 1917.

Chapter Nine

SENTINELS

PRESIDENT-ELECT WOODROW WILSON ARRIVED IN WASHington on March 3, 1913, for his inauguration the next day.

As Wilson stepped off his train, one of his aides looked around and asked, "Where are all the people?"

About five hundred supporters had shown up to greet the nation's new leader. The rest, numbering in the thousands, were lining up less than a mile away for the largest march ever assembled on American soil, one even bigger than the New York City march the previous year.

Alice Paul had a plan for putting voting rights for women at the top of Wilson's new political agenda. Wilson had come to Washington on a tide of popular support, eager to strengthen American democracy in the new century. Alice Paul could not have agreed with him more.

And to begin with, she decided to steal his show.

As the president-elect was making his way to the

nation's capital by train that afternoon, thousands of women were forming ranks carefully on Pennsylvania Avenue in Washington—not to celebrate the president-elect's arrival in town, but to make sure he felt the power of the movement they had built.

They had arrived from all over the country, representing every state and every organization and profession dominated by women. Many wore elaborate costumes. Alice Paul had choreographed the event down to the smallest detail, from the order of the marchers to the floats they accompanied to the hundreds of banners they carried.

On the marble steps of the Treasury Department, a famous dancer named Florence Fleming Noyes, dressed like an ancient Greek goddess, flanked by seven attendants dressed in white, waved gracefully to the crowd. A postcard capturing the image of Noyes, with the caption "Liberty and Her Attendants (Suffragette's Tableau)," was later mailed out to thousands of women who could not attend the march.

All along the route, newspaper photographers took pictures of the marchers, and reporters jotted down animated accounts of the historic event. It was exactly what Alice Paul had in mind.

But as the parade made its way toward the White House, thousands of men, outraged at the very idea that women might vote, heckled and even spit on the marchers. Some of the women became terrified as the men grew violent and pressed in on the parade from both sides of the avenue.

The women had to fight their way forward, with few police officers to protect them.

Alice Paul had asked the chief of police to protect the marchers, but he never responded to her requests. The government, she learned, was not ready to get behind the suffrage movement or even to take women's concerns seriously. By the end of the march, more than one hundred women had to be hospitalized for their injuries.

At the head of the parade, a young woman rode atop a white horse, wearing a cape and a gold crown. There was a star on her crown she called "the star of hope," which was meant to symbolize "the free woman of the future."

She galloped into the crowds of men to try to drive them back from the marchers, displaying a fearlessness that made a powerful impression on all who saw her.

The woman on horseback, Inez Milholland, devoted her life to winning the vote for women.

When Inez married a Dutch man, the United States government stripped her of her US citizenship because according to US law, a woman always had to adopt the citizenship of her husband, whether she wanted to or not. As a citizen of another country, Inez knew that she could not vote in the United States, but as a true champion of women's political equality, her citizenship didn't stop her from devoting all her energies to the suffrage movement.

After the march, Inez kept up her fearless attacks on the opponents of people power. Her total confidence inspired thousands of other women to follow her brave example and join the movement.

By the fall of 1916, Inez had been on the road for weeks, talking to groups around the country and rallying them to the cause of democracy. She was exhausted and suffering from anemia. But she decided to give everything she could to this mission.

"This is the time to fight," she said.

Milholland had given fifty speeches in eight different states over the course of twenty-eight days. In the mining town of Virginia City, Nevada, five hundred people had turned out to hear her.

Finally, on October 23, 1916, Milholland gave a speech in front of a thousand women in Los Angeles, where she urged them to press forward together to achieve the vote. Sick now with tonsillitis and strep throat, she collapsed suddenly onstage. She never recovered. Barely a month later, on her deathbed, Milholland is reported to have said, "Mr. President, how long must women wait for liberty?"

Inez Milholland had died fighting for votes for women, the first American martyr to the suffragists' cause. At her funeral, they vowed to take her battle to the next level.

A short time later, in January 1917, Alice Paul and other members of her recently formed National Woman's Party started a demonstration outside the White House, the first group of activists ever in American history to protest in front of the president's home. It was a media sensation, and a huge embarrassment for President Wilson.

The "picketers," as they were called, appeared at the White House every single day, carrying large banners with messages for the president. Some of these quoted Milholland's words; others threw the president's words back at him: "Mr. President you say 'liberty is the fundamental demand of the human spirit.'"

Neither snow nor rain deterred the protesters, and they kept at it through the winter, spring, and summer of 1917. Thousands of women from different places and different backgrounds added their bodies and messages to the demonstration. By simply showing up every day, standing quietly and holding signs, these women sent shock waves through American politics.

The press dubbed Paul and her group the "Silent

Sentinels." At first, the Silent Sentinels attracted mostly curious onlookers.

By June, however, police officers had begun to harass and even arrest the picketers, charging them with blocking the sidewalk. When the court later fined Alice Paul twenty-five dollars, she announced that "as members of a disfranchised class, we do not recognize a court established by a political officer from whose election women were excluded." Intentionally or not, she was directly echoing the revolutionaries who declared independence from Great Britain in 1776.

Finally, the police grew impatient and hauled Alice Paul and her sister protesters off to jail.

"We are being imprisoned," Paul quipped cleverly to the reporters who covered her case, "not because we obstructed traffic, but because we pointed out to the President the fact that he was obstructing the cause of democracy at home, while Americans were fighting for it abroad" in World War I.

For the next several months, Alice Paul and other protesters languished behind bars at the Occoquan Workhouse in Virginia, just south of the nation's capital. Though they insisted that they were political prisoners, jailed for their beliefs, the authorities treated them as criminals.

Their food was infested with maggots; rats scampered across the floors.

In November, Alice Paul and Rose Winslow went on a hunger strike, refusing all food, to call attention to their cause. In response, prison staff force-fed them three times a day, through tubes forced down their throats. Prison authorities, and the US government, believed they could break the will of the suffragists.

On the night of November 14, prison guards at Occoquan subjected the women to what survivors called the "Night of Terror." Lucy Burns, who cofounded the National Woman's Party, was forced to stand all night with her hands manacled to her jail cell bars, high above her head. Guards slammed Dorothy Day, who later became a renowned Catholic social activist and candidate for sainthood, against her metal bed frame. Other women were clubbed and beaten; one suffered a heart attack.

The government seemed to be willing to go to almost any length to stop the women's suffrage movement. By sending the Silent Sentinels to jail, the local authorities may have believed that they had doused the fires of rebellion. Exactly the opposite happened.

News of the violent treatment of Paul and the suffragists sparked a wave of outrage across the United States and a nationwide movement to secure their release.

They went right back to the White House gates. In the winter of 1918, the Silent Sentinels installed a portable fire pit, which they kept lit at all times. As a symbolic gesture (and as reporters looked on), they burned copies of every word President Wilson had spoken about democracy.

"We had an enormous bell," Alice Paul recalled, "and every time Wilson would make one of these speeches, we would toll this great bell, and then somebody would go outside with the President's speech and, with great dignity, burn it in our little caldron."

Finally, after years of putting pressure on President Wilson, the suffrage movement won him over. On September 30, 1918, the president announced his support for a constitutional amendment giving women the right to vote.

On June 4, 1919, Congress passed the Nineteenth Amendment:

> The right of citizens of the United States to vote shall not be denied or abridged by the United States or by any State on account of sex.
>
> Congress shall have power to enforce this article by appropriate legislation.

The biggest battle of all lay ahead.

In order for the Nineteenth Amendment to become part of the Constitution, it had to be ratified by three-fourths of the states, which in 1919 amounted to thirty-six of the forty-eight states.

The women of the suffrage movement had come to Washington to persuade a president; now they took their battle to the states, one by one. They showed up on street corners and spoke eloquently. They debated the merits of their cause in their homes and in churches. They crowded the steps of town halls and statehouses. And in state after state, they made sure that the Nineteenth Amendment would be ratified.

In one fell swoop, the Nineteenth Amendment added more voters to the United States than any other single act in American history.

Women did not simply "get the vote" when the Nineteenth Amendment finally went into effect in August 1920. They had imagined a different country, fought for it, and made that dream a reality.

Mary Church Terrell, civil rights and suffrage activist, in the late nineteenth century.

Chapter Ten

SIDELINED

WHEN ALICE PAUL AND THE LEADERS OF THE SUFFRAGE movement held their final convention to celebrate the Nineteenth Amendment, a group of Black women reached out to ask for help in their fight against the many barriers that women of color still faced in a racially segregated America. After all, even after the Nineteenth Amendment passed, Black women could still not vote in the South, where most of them lived.

Paul and her white allies declined the request. After the convention, the all-white leadership of the movement for votes for women declared their work finished.

Never mind the decades of voting-rights activism, the successful ratification of a constitutional amendment, or the amendment's promise that "the right of citizens of the United States to vote shall not be denied or abridged by the United States or by any State on account of sex."

The fact was that most women still could not vote. The story of voting rights in America has never followed a straight line or a single path. Even today, many students learn that the suffrage movement won the vote for women— period. But the truth is that African American, immigrant, and Native women across the United States had arrived by a different route, and had a longer road to travel. Their way was blocked by racism, discrimination, and laws that specifically excluded them from casting a ballot.

For women of color, the Nineteenth Amendment was the beginning, not the end, of their quest. Their voting-rights struggle continued.

Ever since Reconstruction, Black women had gone after the right to vote no less passionately than white women. They founded the National Association of Colored Women in 1896 to pull Black women into politics at a time when white supremacy was hardening all across the United States. The NACW's first president, Mary Church Terrell, fought for voting rights for all women—even when the suffrage movement's leaders and members sought to exclude African American women from their cause.

In some ways, Black and white women faced similar challenges, as all women confronted sexism at home and in public. But Black women were also fighting a wider, more dangerous battle against lynching, racial segregation, both legal and unofficial, and the new campaign to remove Black people from politics in the South.

Now, the same dirty tricks that prevented Black men from voting in the South applied directly to Black women as well. In Mississippi, news of the Nineteenth Amendment's ratification prompted state lawmakers to change their poll tax rule: Now Black women were legally required to pay it as well, a fact that would keep many of them away from the polls.

For Black suffragists, going to jail—or even speaking in public—could be deadly.

Terrell and the NACW understood the unique need and the special power of an organization led by Black women. "Our peculiar status in this country," Terrell said, "seems to demand that we stand by ourselves."

It was a lesson born of long and sometimes painful experience with their white allies. For example, some white suffrage leaders had wanted to exclude Black women from the Washington, DC, suffrage march entirely, for fear of offending the Southern white suffragists who supported racial segregation in their home states. Some Black women eventually pressured Paul to let them join—but they were mostly ignored by the media.

(The gutsy equal rights crusader Ida B. Wells refused

to risk such second-class treatment. She waited on the sidelines until the Illinois delegation of white suffragists from her home state passed by, at which point she simply stepped into the line, her head held high.)

Other women of color found themselves similarly left behind by a movement, and a constitutional amendment, that promised political equality for all women.

Mabel Ping-Hua Lee attended Barnard College and went on to earn her PhD in economics from Columbia University in 1921, the first Chinese American woman in the United States to earn a doctorate. Although she dreamed of returning to China to support the democracy movement there, when her father died in 1924, she took over his ministry and spent the rest of her life serving her community in Chinatown. Mabel made the trip to China three times before the outbreak of civil war there in 1927, when travel became risky and the United States' restrictions on Chinese travelers made reentering the country difficult.

Even when the Nineteenth Amendment was ratified and granted American women the right to vote, women like Lee remained on the outside, banned from voting because of the Chinese Exclusion Act.

Chinese-born American women—and men—would

have to wait. They could not vote until 1943, when Congress finally repealed the Chinese Exclusion Act. There is no record of Mabel Ping-Hua Lee voting in her lifetime.

When women gained the right to vote in 1920, Zitkála-Šá directly appealed to her white sisters to support Native Americans in their own struggle for full citizenship. Like Black suffragists, she, too, was rebuffed. But she never gave up the fight.

In 1924, the US Congress finally responded to pressure from many different quarters and passed the Indian Citizenship Act. After nearly 150 years of being denied representation in their own homeland, it was a dramatic turn in the long journey of Native peoples across the history of the United States:

> **All non-citizen Indians born within the territorial limits of the United States be, and they are hereby, declared to be citizens of the United States.**

The white legislators who passed the act believed that this was the end of the matter. But Native people all over the United States knew better. Like African Americans, they saw that when a flame of equal rights burned in Washington, DC, its bright light rarely shone across all the states equally. In many places, especially where Native Americans lived in large numbers, the fact of citizenship did not yet translate into the right to vote.

It took forty more years for all Native Americans to gain the right to vote, even though federal law had decided that they were equal citizens.

Fifteen years after the Indian Citizenship Act, Native Americans still could not vote in Maine. As one man reported in the late 1930s, "the Indians aren't allowed to have a voice in state affairs because they aren't voters." Before 1948, Native people in New Mexico were barred from voting because they did not pay state taxes as residents of reservations—onto which they had been forced by the government in the first place. In 1956, the Utah Supreme Court decided that Native Americans could not vote because they were incapable of being good citizens.

Many Native people achieved the right to vote only *very* recently. South Dakota blocked Native Americans from voting by law until the 1940s, but in some counties, local courts and poll workers would not let Native people vote until as late as the 1970s—a century after Zitkála-Šá's birth.

On February 15, 1921, representatives from the National Woman's Party gathered in the US Capitol to unveil a new statue dedicated to "our three pioneers of suffrage." When the cloth was pulled from the statue, it revealed three white women cast in bronze: Elizabeth Cady Stanton, Lucretia Mott, and Susan B. Anthony.

No one else was commemorated that day. Black and brown women, immigrant women, Native women: All had put their lives on the line for voting rights, and it seemed that their stories were already being whitewashed from the historical record.

In Alabama, New York, South Dakota, New Mexico, Hawaii, and many other corners of the United States, these women carried the fight forward at a time when voting rights were off the table for anyone but white Americans.

In 1917, the same year that women in New York won the right to vote, a Black woman named Fannie Lou Hamer was born into dire poverty in Ruleville, Mississippi. She lived on a former cotton plantation and began picking cotton herself at the age of thirteen instead of attending school.

Fannie Lou Hamer was as powerless as any American at that point in the nation's history. But after a life lived under the heel of white supremacy, she was destined to lead the nation into a new era of people power: our own.

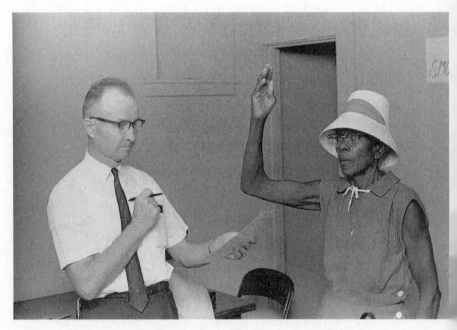

Seventy-year-old Joe Ella Moore takes the oath of registration for the first time in her life at the Magnolia Motel in Prentiss, Mississippi, on August 25, 1965.

Chapter Eleven

FREEDOM

EVER SINCE THEY STOLE THE RIGHT TO VOTE FROM BLACK people, white Southerners believed they had built an unshakable system to keep democracy out. White elected officials in statehouses and in Congress made sure no law was passed to interfere with their power. And white sheriffs, courthouse officials, and vigilantes made sure Black Southerners stayed away from the voting booth.

Black Southerners, however, didn't give up. In the 1930s, local branches of the NAACP mounted a legal campaign against Jim Crow, trying to chip away at the laws that kept African Americans powerless. "We want only one thing, primarily," a Black man from Mississippi wrote the NAACP, "that is the ballot."

In 1944, NAACP lawyers won a major victory with *Smith v. Allwright*, a Supreme Court case that declared the "white" primary unconstitutional. Primaries are elections run by political parties to determine the candidates they will put up for office. Until the Supreme Court's decision, political parties could create their own rules about who could vote—and they openly limited their primaries to whites only, virtually guaranteeing that only white candidates could ever run for election. By outlawing this practice, the Supreme Court made it possible for Black Southerners to participate in primaries for the first time. Poll taxes and literacy tests still remained in place—but the court had opened a door, and thousands of African Americans were determined to march through it.

After World War II—a war fought by Americans in the name of freedom—a new generation of brave activists decided that it was time to bring democracy home. More than a million African Americans had served in the military, and their service had given them a fresh sense of power and purpose. Many of them had no intention of returning to the United States and submitting to Jim Crow. During the war, they had campaigned under the banner of the "Double V": victory overseas against the enemy, and victory over segregation and racism at home.

In 1946, a Black war veteran named Medgar Evers, along with his brother Charles, returned home to Mississippi and decided to register new Black voters. White vigilantes threatened Evers at his home—just as Klansmen had attacked Black voters during Reconstruction.

In Georgia, the Army veteran Maceo Snipes became the first African American ever to cast a vote in Taylor County. The next day, four white men murdered him in front of his home.

Voting-rights activism was dangerous, but thousands of veterans like Evers and Snipes were willing to put their lives on the line for the ballot. In local communities all over the South, they discovered that the fires of Reconstruction had never gone out. With each passing year, these new people-power heroes kindled them once again.

In the 1950s, the Civil Rights Movement burst onto the national scene when a group of ordinary citizens in Montgomery, Alabama, refused to ride on the segregated buses that carried them to and from work each day. The Montgomery bus boycott snowballed into different campaigns across the South. Through dogged organizing, legal brilliance, and courageous protests, a new generation of freedom fighters achieved victories over segregated schools, lunch counters, and public transportation—places where for generations Black people had felt the sting and experienced the humiliation of racial oppression and second-class status.

At every step in the struggle for civil rights, African Americans met fierce resistance from the white South. But nothing triggered a response more stubborn or violent than the campaign for the vote.

White Southerners launched a campaign of terror against Black voters, tightening the vise that was the main source of white control over Black people. It was already incredibly difficult for a Black person to vote in many places, but states like Mississippi, Alabama, and Georgia decided to make it just about impossible.

African Americans who attempted to register to vote lost their jobs. They received death threats at home, at work, and in school. And white vigilantes terrorized them with hateful violence.

Two weeks after the Reverend George W. Lee spoke in support of voting rights during a rally at the all-Black town of Mound Bayou, Mississippi, he was gunned down by white vigilantes while driving home. Six months later, a sixty-five-year-old voting-rights activist named Gus Courts nearly died of gunshot wounds sustained while working in his grocery store; he left the state for Chicago when he recovered. After a World War II veteran named Lamar Smith encouraged his neighbors in the town of Brookhaven to vote, he was found dead in the middle of the town's main street. Even though witnesses had seen a specific white man walking away covered in blood, the police never arrested anyone for the murder.

The new assault on democracy seemed to work. Over half a million Black Mississippians were old enough and eligible to vote in 1955, and with the help of activists like Medgar Evers, twenty-two thousand African Americans had succeeded in registering. Two years later, that number had fallen by half. In many Black-majority counties in the state, not a single Black person was registered to vote.

But as the number of voting-rights casualties grew, Black Southerners hardened their determination to bring democracy to the South. In the 1960s, all over the South, Black people and their white allies risked their lives to get back the vote.

Their white opponents were just as determined to keep it away.

In 1963, a white supremacist shot Medgar Evers dead in front of his home in Jackson, Mississippi.

White Southerners believed that they could push Black people back down.

Instead, a new voting-rights movement exploded in the one place where it seemed least likely to succeed. Its new leader showed America how the simple act of voting could transform powerlessness into a new wave of people power.

In the early 1960s, Fannie Lou Hamer lived not far from where she was born, in a rented shack on a cotton plantation in Sunflower County, Mississippi, a place entirely controlled by a small group of white people who ruthlessly dominated their Black workers.

Fewer than 1 percent of Black people in Sunflower County could vote, even though they made up a large majority of the population. This meant that African Americans had no say over the police, the schools, the courts, or the county government that controlled nearly every part of their lives. They were poor, and powerless. By preventing Black people from voting, the white minority in Sunflower County (including the powerful US senator James O. Eastland, who owned a cotton plantation there) had held on to power since the late nineteenth century.

"I had never heard, until 1962, that black people could register and vote," Hamer said.

That year, she learned about voting from a group of activists from the Student Nonviolent Coordinating Committee (SNCC, pronounced "snick"), who had come to her hometown of Ruleville to educate local people about how to register to vote. She immediately warmed up to the

young men, who persuaded her to join them in their campaign to bring voting rights to Mississippi.

In no time, she became one of the group's most effective leaders.

"You know the ballot is good," Fannie Lou once said.
"If it wasn't good, how come he trying to keep you from it
and he still using it?"

Hamer endured beatings and threats, and she was even
kicked out of her home on the plantation. But she had made
a decision to help her people and she never wavered from it.

In the fall of 1963, Black Mississippians tried to prove a
point about the lack of true democracy in their state by
holding a huge, statewide mock election. Over eighty
thousand people, most of them African American, voted
in a pretend election for governor.

They called it a "freedom vote."

Hamer and her fellow activists believed that they could
show Mississippi, and America, what democracy looked
like. But now they confronted a bigger question: How could
they achieve real political power? How could they take
their democracy campaign a step further? In the spring of
1964, they decided to take it on the road—literally.

There was a presidential election that year. Both national political parties—the Democrats and the Republicans—held their nominating conventions in the summer to choose which candidate would make a run for the White House. Every state, including Mississippi, sent elected delegates to the convention.

Every one of the Mississippi delegates was white, because in Mississippi, Democratic Party officials refused to allow Black people to vote.

Hamer and a new organization called the Mississippi Freedom Democratic Party decided that this would be the perfect opportunity to speak up for Mississippians who had no say in choosing their candidate for president. They set up meetings across the state and held local elections for delegates, inviting anyone, of any color, to participate. In June, these Freedom Democrats took their campaign to a national stage, when they sent their *own* delegation to the Democratic National Convention in Atlantic City, New Jersey, and demanded to be recognized as the true representatives of their state.

Just a few years earlier, Hamer had toiled in the cotton fields six days a week. On August 22, 1964, at the Democratic National Convention, Hamer spoke for the Freedom Democrats in front of a televised audience of millions.

She called out the hypocrisy of a system that celebrated democracy for some but denied it for all.

"We want to register, to become first-class citizens," Hamer said. "And if the Freedom Democratic Party is not seated now, I question America. Is this America, the land of the free and the home of the brave?"

The Democratic Party refused to acknowledge the Freedom Democrats as legitimate representatives of Mississippi voters. But the democracy movement they helped to create was unstoppable.

On Sunday, March 7, 1965, six hundred people gathered in Selma, Alabama, to march across the Edmund Pettus Bridge to Montgomery, to demonstrate for federal legislation to protect the right to vote. As they crossed over, local and state policemen charged into the peaceful marchers with whips, clubs, and guns, seriously injuring hundreds of men and women, including the young SNCC leader John Lewis. (Lewis later narrated this story in his graphic memoir, *March*).

The violence caught on news cameras shocked the nation. The protesters left President Johnson no choice but to act. By putting their lives on the line, they broke through the white South's wall of "massive resistance."

On August 6, the president signed the Voting Rights Act. "An act to enforce the fifteenth amendment to the

Constitution," the Voting Rights Act outlawed racial discrimination at the voting booth and gave the federal government extensive powers to ensure that Americans could vote without interference.

That night, the president spoke to a televised audience of more than seventy million Americans. "This act flows from a clear and simple wrong," he said. "Its only purpose is to right that wrong. Millions of Americans are denied the right to vote because of their color. This law will ensure them the right to vote."

As John Lewis later said, "The right to vote is precious, almost sacred. It is the most powerful nonviolent tool or instrument in a democratic society. We must use it."

A short time later, Joe Ella Moore registered to vote in a motel in Prentiss, Mississippi, with the help of federal officials sent there following the passage of the Voting Rights Act. She had shown up after hearing on the radio that President Johnson had signed a law making it legal for all people to vote. Moore had already attempted to register *seven times* throughout her life, and had been turned away each time. Now, at seventy years old, she succeeded in adding her name to the rolls of voters, the first in a new wave of people ready to step forward and bring democracy to the South.

The Voting Rights Act remains the bedrock of our democracy. By affirming that no state has the right to create rules or laws that keep anyone away from the polls, the act finally solved the problem that the Founding Fathers created when they drafted the original Constitution.

The Voting Rights Act had been drafted by officials in Washington, but it was made possible by ordinary people across the South who refused to accept anything less than their constitutional rights as citizens of the United States.

As far as they were concerned, people power was now the American way.

A sign in Lowndes County, Alabama, encouraging African Americans to vote for the Lowndes County Freedom Organization, whose symbol was the black panther.

JIM PEPPLER, PHOTOGRAPHER, ALABAMA DEPARTMENT OF ARCHIVES AND HISTORY

Chapter Twelve

THE BLACK PANTHER

A YOUNG SNCC ACTIVIST NAMED STOKELY CARMICHAEL arrived in Lowndes County, Alabama, on March 23, 1965. SNCC had decided to come to Lowndes to support local African Americans who were attempting to register to vote.

Only two days later, a civil rights activist named Viola Liuzzo was murdered in Selma, Alabama, by a carload of white supremacists who fired on the car she was driving.

Over 80 percent of the residents of Lowndes County were African American, but in 1965, only one Black person was registered to vote. White people intended to keep it that way.

Known as "Bloody Lowndes," it was a dangerous place to fight for voting rights.

At twenty-three years old, Stokely Carmichael was already becoming one of the most famous leaders of the

Civil Rights Movement. He joined SNCC while an under-graduate at Howard University and participated in the Freedom Rides in the summer of 1961, in which dozens of Black students and activists (among them John Lewis) rode in buses across the South to challenge segregated bus stations, restrooms, and water fountains. He was thrown in prison that summer for trying to desegregate a lunch counter in Mississippi. Carmichael was charming, brave, and intelligent, and had a natural ability to talk with people of many different backgrounds. Through months of hard work and many miles walking the dirt roads of Lowndes County, he made a deep connection with the Black community.

A SNCC flyer plastered on doors and fence posts around Lowndes County made his case clearly:

> Now is the time! If ever we had a chance to do something about the years of low pay, beatings, burnings of homes, denial of the right to vote, bad education and washed-out roads—Now is the time!

Stokely Carmichael and his fellow SNCC organizers believed that the true power of the vote was not simply in choosing a president, senators, or representatives, as important as these elected offices were. American democracy then and now has many layers, and citizens have many different opportunities to vote for the representatives whose decisions shape their everyday lives.

Carmichael understood that white supremacy, the system designed to keep Black people powerless, depended on a network of local officeholders. The decisions made by these officeholders, day in and day out, were the invisible glue that held racial inequality together.

Elected school board members determined budgets and what could be taught. (Would Black students be taught that all people are equal? Would Black-majority schools receive enough funding?) Elected sheriffs decided how the laws would be enforced. (Would Black people be unfairly targeted by police?) Elected judges decided how the laws would be interpreted. (Would African Americans be sentenced to jail more often than white people?) In Lowndes County, even the tax collector was elected by local voters. (Would Black and white residents be taxed equally?)

Voting shaped every stage in a person's life. In a county where the majority of the population was Black but only white people could vote, this meant that unfairness was built into the system, from the cradle to the grave.

SNCC's aim was to teach Lowndes County's Black majority how to unravel this system from the ground up.

One of Carmichael's fellow SNCC members, a brilliant activist named Courtland Cox, argued that "when you have a situation where the community is 80 percent black, why complain about police brutality when you can be the sheriff yourself? Why complain about substandard education when you could be the Board of Education? Why complain about the courthouse when you could move to take it over yourself? [In] places where you could exercise the control, why complain about it? Why protest when you can exercise power?"

Carmichael agreed. The key to getting rid of white supremacy in Lowndes County was making sure that Black people were free to exercise their right to vote.

Without the help of outsiders, and inspired by news of the movement in Selma, Alabama, local people in Lowndes County had already been organizing voter registration drives in the spring of 1965. The arrival of SNCC volunteers supercharged their efforts by adding know-how and connections to that local campaign.

Carmichael and his fellow organizers walked country roads, going door-to-door and visiting with people who had never participated in any election or political process. They told people about the Voting Rights Act and explained to them what rights all Americans had.

Local registrars came up with new tricks to turn back the new movement for democracy. They would challenge people's home addresses or the correct spelling of their names; they would send them home for additional paperwork when none was legally required.

By one estimate, as many as half of all Black residents of Lowndes County were rejected by the registrars that summer, either for minor technical reasons, or for no reason at all. For some, the constant stonewalling became discouraging. "We just couldn't keep bringing the same people down over and over," Stokely Carmichael said.

But African Americans, one by one or in small groups, kept coming.

SNCC succeeded in persuading several thousand lawfully registered Black residents of Lowndes County to show up to vote. That alone was a historic accomplishment. But their work went deeper: The simple act of gathering people together to talk about voting and democracy was nothing short of...revolutionary. Black people had not gathered in Lowndes County to talk about voting for a long, long time—not since the end of Reconstruction, in fact. Not since the vote had been stolen from them. Not since the door had closed on democracy in the South.

History was coming full circle. The Second Reconstruction was coming to Lowndes County.

By the end of 1965, more than half of all registered voters in Lowndes County were African American. The question remained for the county's Black voters: How would they make use of their new voting power?

Carmichael and his allies saw a problem. Ever since the violent overthrow of Reconstruction, there had been only one party in the South, the Democratic Party. Although the Democrats, on the national level, had supported the cause of civil rights, the southern wing of the party had systematically excluded Black people and helped maintain white supremacy. Choosing between two Democratic candidates would be like choosing the lesser of two evils for Black voters—a lose-lose proposition. How could Black voters, in good conscience, support the very party that had oppressed them for nearly a century?

The only answer was to create a party of their own: the Lowndes County Freedom Organization. Carmichael also wanted to inspire local people with a new symbol, one that clearly expressed the awakening of people power in Lowndes County. He chose an iconic creature that was thought to stalk the woods of Alabama: the black panther.

"The black panther is an animal that when it is pressured it moves back until it is cornered, then it comes out fighting for life or death," said a local Freedom Organization activist.

On Election Day in November 1966, the weapons of white supremacy were on display. Armed white men stalked some polling places, menacing any Black person who approached. White plantation owners loaded up buses with their Black employees, and then handed them ballots with the names of white candidates already filled in. White bosses even entered voting booths to intimidate Black workers into voting their way. One SNCC worker spotted near a polling place was nearly beaten to death by a white mob.

All of this was a year *after* the passage of the Voting Rights Act, which was supposed to protect the right of all people to vote in the United States. Black people realized that the law wasn't going to hand them the vote. They were going to have to fight for it.

Despite the threats, and in the face of open intimidation, hundreds of Black voters turned up at the polls anyway and cast their votes for the Freedom Organization candidate. The image of the black panther gave them strength. A voter named Maggie Connors commented, "I pulled that lever till the black cat howled."

When the votes were counted, however, Lowndes

County remained in the grip of white supremacy. The county clerks and election officials—the same people in charge of counting the votes—were all white Democrats. They had no plans to let go of their power.

But the Freedom Organization and the black panther had kindled a spark inside the Black community of Lowndes County. Having been powerless for almost a century leading up to this Election Day, they now felt the power of the vote.

In 1970, voters elected John Hulett, the first Freedom Organization chairperson, as sheriff—the first Black person elected to office in Lowndes County since Reconstruction. Black people still remembered being terrorized by white sheriffs who enforced the color line in Lowndes with violence and impunity. This simple shift dramatically transformed everyday life in Lowndes County for African Americans.

Other victories followed. By 1978, Black candidates had been elected to the offices of judge, coroner, county clerk, school board member, and tax assessor, among many others. As just one example of the many ways this improved life for African American citizens, the newly elected Black tax assessor discovered that white landowners had not been paying their fair share of county taxes, while African Americans had always been taxed at the highest rate possible, a problem he fixed right away.

Life did not change for the Black majority of Lowndes County overnight; with each new election, African Americans had to work to make it real. But the black panther cast a long shadow, a symbol of when they stepped forward and reclaimed their rightful power.

Willie Velásquez (left) examines a voting map of San Antonio, Texas, in 1982.

Chapter Thirteen

VOICE

OUTSIDE THE SOUTH, OTHER CHARACTERS IN THIS DRAMA waged their own campaigns for democracy on the streets of New York, in the borderlands of the Southwest, and in the sprawling cities and towns of the West Coast. People fighting for the same rights did not always live in the same places, or even speak the same language.

In 1974, the Southwest Voter Registration Education Project in San Antonio, Texas, was nothing but a table, two folding chairs (one occupied by Willie Velásquez, the organization's only employee at the time), and a telephone. Until that point, Velásquez was a one-person operation, with a big dream and a small bank account. (The one-room office was a step up from the SVREP's first address, which happened to be Willie's apartment, where he lived with his wife and newborn son.) But his imagination was much bigger than the project's cramped, haphazard headquarters.

Velásquez had a reputation as a fighter, someone who wasn't afraid to speak up for his people, the millions of Mexican Americans who made the Southwest their home. He had spent his college years as a student activist in Texas, speaking up for Mexican American rights. At twenty-five, he met John Lewis, the chairman and cofounder of SNCC, who convinced him that voting was the key to people power. From that point onward, he dedicated his life to a single goal.

Velásquez dreamed of building "the biggest voter registration organization the Mexican community had ever seen." By registering hundreds of thousands of new voters, he would do something no one had ever attempted: build Latino political power in the United States.

"Su voto es su voz," he said. Your vote is your voice.

All over the Southwest, Mexican Americans found themselves fenced in by racial discrimination and segregation. Mexican American children attended separate, underfunded schools and lived with their families in separate, Spanish-speaking neighborhoods. Train stations, movie theaters, and restaurants forced Mexican Americans to sit in separate sections—or denied them entry altogether. And poll taxes and literacy tests kept Mexican Americans from voting—which meant that mayors, judges, and sheriffs were nearly always white.

African Americans lived for nearly a century under the harsh rules of Jim Crow; some Mexican Americans in the Southwest renamed that system Juan Crow.

Velásquez was Juan Crow's sworn enemy. But he also noticed something in the hours and days he spent going door-to-door in Mexican American neighborhoods, where few, if any, people were registered to vote. His people weren't even *trying* to register, he realized. It was as if they had given up.

When he dug deeper, however, Velásquez learned that the whole voting system was designed to keep Mexican Americans away. Districts were drawn to make it impossible for Mexican American candidates to win elections. In some areas, election officials conducted purges of voter rolls, removing the names of Mexican Americans. Some towns even had separate ballot boxes for white voters and Mexican Americans, whose votes would mysteriously disappear. And literacy tests discriminated against Spanish speakers.

White politicians did nothing to help the Mexican Americans they represented. Velásquez realized that it was no great mystery why his people didn't vote. The system told them that their votes—their voices—simply didn't matter. No wonder they stayed away.

His challenge, then, was not only to register more

voters from his community. It was also to persuade them to get involved and even get elected themselves. Mexican Americans needed their own voice, their own spokespeople, and their own political power.

Velásquez realized that to get his message out, he had to go where his community was reading and listening. Using specially prepared research, he learned that most Mexican Americans were deeply connected to the world around them and aware of what was going on in American politics—but all through their own Spanish-language newspapers, magazines, radio, and television. This was an entirely different linguistic world right under the noses of the white politicians who held all the political power in the Southwest. They simply paid no attention to it.

"If we [Mexican Americans] started a revolution tomorrow and announced it on Spanish radio," Velásquez once said, "we'd be the only ones to know it was happening."

Velásquez saw an opportunity. Spanish language had been used as an excuse for keeping Mexican Americans away from politics. Instead, Velásquez believed that it could be a tool to draw them in. Language could be the source of the power, not an obstacle to getting it.

In Fort Bend County, near the city of Houston, well

over a quarter of the population was Mexican American, but very few of them had registered to vote. Only one Mexican American person had ever been elected to public office in the county's history. Most of its Mexican American citizens were poor, and powerless.

Velásquez and his SVREP staff arrived in 1975.

They composed a traditional song, called a corrido, celebrating "El Despierto de Fort Bend" (The Awakening of Fort Bend), which became wildly popular during the campaign. The song told the story of the Mexican American community of Fort Bend finding its voice and its strength.

"¡Despierte! ¡Regístrese! ¡Y Vote!" (Wake up! Register! And Vote!)

They conducted interviews with political candidates in the local Spanish-language newspaper and insisted that they talk about the issues that Mexican Americans cared about—such as bilingual education in the schools, better streets, and services for their children.

At local community meetings, high school students organized traditional Mexican dances and sang songs in Spanish.

All of this showed the people of Fort Bend that to grab hold of their power as American citizens, they did not have to let go of who they were. It was a simple lesson with a convincing outcome: When Velásquez and his fellow organizers had finished their work, more than two thousand local residents had registered to vote, an increase of over *60 percent*. And that fall, they elected the first Mexican American judge in the county's history.

"There is no question that we are participating in an historical awakening of Chicanos throughout the [region and the nation]," Velásquez said. "Everywhere our people are beginning to question old injustices and working to improve ourselves through the ballot box."

Velásquez and his fellow organizers at SVREP were creating a new democracy movement among Mexican Americans. In the late 1970s and early 1980s, this movement flowed into other voter registration efforts in the Midwest and among Puerto Ricans and other Spanish-speaking communities in the Northeast. They combined forces into the National Hispanic Voter Registration Campaign, which targeted millions of new potential voters. Together, they were generating a new political force in American politics, one that was both unashamedly bilingual and proudly American.

In the Southwest alone, more than 2.7 million Hispanic voters had registered to vote by the mid-1980s, a huge surge since the years when Velásquez began his work. It was a leap forward in people power as big as Reconstruction, women's suffrage, or the Civil Rights Movement. Latinos in cities as varied as Miami, Chicago, New York, Seattle, Phoenix, and Los Angeles were carrying the story of democracy forward, continuing the fight begun during the American Revolution.

On June 15, 1988, Willie Velásquez's democracy work was cut short when he died from cancer at only forty-four years old. According to his brother, his final words were "qué bonito es el nuevo mundo." The new world is so beautiful.

Part Three

TWO ROADS

A HUNDRED YEARS AFTER ROBERT SMALLS escaped across Confederate lines, the Voting Rights Act picked up where Reconstruction left off. Some even called it America's "Second Reconstruction."

Just to make sure, the Voting Rights Act gave special powers to the federal government. A state wanting to change its voting laws had to check with the Department of Justice first. Known as "preclearance," this rule forced the government to keep its promises to local people everywhere.

For once, ordinary people of all backgrounds seemed to hold the cards. They had the law on their side, and they voted—by the millions.

But people power's old enemies weren't ready to give up yet. They shifted tactics. They spun new myths about the dangers of democracy. They invented new tricks to keep people away from the polls.

Ordinary people didn't take these challenges sitting down. They made sure that the fight for people power, America's democracy story, would continue.

Maggie Bozeman speaking about voting rights in Tuskegee, Alabama, in 1982.

Chapter Fourteen

DIRTY TRICKS

In June 1981, almost sixteen years after the Voting Rights Act became law, a fifty-year-old schoolteacher named Maggie Bozeman showed up to testify before a subcommittee of the United States House of Representatives. The group had traveled to Montgomery, Alabama, to hold hearings on voting rights in a Southern state where memories of the Civil Rights Movement and voter suppression— at least among Black Southerners—were still fresh.

Bozeman taught second grade in Aliceville, Alabama, a rural town that was over 40 percent African American. But she was also one of Aliceville's natural leaders, a person who spoke up at school board meetings, protested for better pay for municipal workers, and prodded city hall into paving the roads on her side of town, where most of Aliceville's Black residents lived. A lawyer for the NAACP named Lani Guinier (who later became an influential defender of voting rights and a professor at Harvard Law School) once described Maggie Bozeman as someone who "changed the weather in the room when she walked in."

"She was like a tornado," Guinier said.

As the president of the Pickens County NAACP chapter, Maggie Bozeman also did everything in her power to make sure that Black people in her home county voted in each election. Somehow, though, no Black candidate had ever been elected to countywide office.

To explain how that could happen, Bozeman painted a dark picture for the members of Congress that day.

To begin with, Alabamans could only register to vote between 8:00 AM and 4:00 PM, which made it almost impossible for people with regular day jobs to show up. When any Black person applied for an absentee ballot (a mail-in ballot often used by people who are away on Election Day), white sheriff's deputies would show up to confirm that they were really not home. Anyone (including Bozeman) assisting an illiterate or elderly person at the polls was photographed by the police and accused of voter fraud; Bozeman had even been arrested for doing this for her neighbors. Lastly, voters in Pickens County were still required to mark their ballots in the open, in full view of election officials and police—a form of voter intimidation that had long been outlawed by the Voting Rights Act.

The laws in Alabama had changed since the era of Jim Crow. But for many people, voting was not much easier than it had been before the Voting Rights Act.

"Just being a voter in Pickens County is a wearying experience," Bozeman said.

Though she was talking about a small rural town in Alabama, Maggie Bozeman could have been describing many places in the United States. From coast to coast, voting is still "a wearying experience" for millions of people, especially people of color.

People like Maggie Bozeman, along with hundreds of thousands of others, worked hard to turn the victories of the Civil Rights Movement into permanent democracy for all Americans. But since the end of Jim Crow, the enemies of democracy had found new ways to undermine the Voting Rights Act, with a grab bag of dirty tricks.

Unlike the American Revolution, the women's suffrage movement, or the Civil Rights Movement, however, this new fight for representation rarely makes the headlines. At times, it's invisible to all but the people closest to the heat of battle. Still, the stakes today are as high as they have ever been.

In 2010, an author and lawyer named Michelle Alexander discovered a shocking attack on our democracy that was hiding in plain sight.

In her bestselling book *The New Jim Crow*, she revealed that in the United States, almost *five million* people of voting age cannot vote because at some point in their lives, they had committed felonies and were sent to prison. Forty-eight states prevent ex-felons from voting through laws which, in some cases, date back to the end of Reconstruction.

"Felon disenfranchisement," as this is called, affects African Americans most of all. Nationwide, nearly one in five Black people cannot vote because of past convictions. Many of these people have already served their time, paid their fines, or otherwise served their court-ordered sentences. Yet they are still marked as criminals, forced to live as second-class citizens without a political voice.

Alexander argues that it's no accident that this new form of Jim Crow took off right after the old one had been destroyed by the efforts of people like Stokely Carmichael, Fannie Lou Hamer, and millions of Black Southerners. The new system, she argues, specifically targets Black people—a form of racial control that only seems to be color-blind. In the 1970s and 1980s, cities and states sent millions of people to prison as a result of new drug laws requiring long sentences for even minor offenses. The prison population soared, reaching heights never seen in any country in history. As a result, the voting population drastically shrank.

The fight against what Alexander calls "mass incarceration" is one of the new fronts in the struggle for voting rights in twenty-first-century America. Inspired by Michelle Alexander's work, a new generation of activists has lobbied state legislators to restore voting rights to formerly incarcerated people.

"Against all odds," Alexander says, "we might find a way to build a multiracial, multiethnic democracy that truly honors the dignity and value of us all."

In 2018, a man named James Baiye II showed up to vote in the same polling place, at a church near Atlanta, where he had voted his entire adult life. When he reached the front of the line, however, Baiye learned that his name was no longer on the voter list—and so he could not vote that morning. The state of Georgia, under a new policy, had decided to "purge" Baiye's name from the voter rolls. The state had done the same thing to more than half a million Georgians that year.

"I wasn't alone in this," he said. "What the heck is going on?"

The explanation was a new form of voter suppression—one that heavily targets areas where people of color are in the majority.

Nine states in America actively purge their voter rolls, silently knocking people off the lists for any number of reasons: errors or misspellings on their registration forms, outdated addresses, or if they haven't voted in a recent election (something that is entirely legal in the United States). When those people show up on Election Day, it's usually too late to reregister, so they are not able to cast a ballot.

The number of purged voters in the United States can be shocking: Georgia removed 1.4 million voters from election lists over an eight-year period. Ohio was about to wipe 235,000 voters from the rolls in 2019 when democracy activists objected. State officials later discovered that forty thousand of the names didn't belong on the purge list in the first place; they had been placed there by accident.

Purging voter rolls is an old trick in the United States. It has been used throughout history to prevent immigrants, African Americans, and sometimes even members of the opposite party from participating in an election. Today, however, this effort to curb our democracy is done in the name of "cleaning" our electoral system and preventing people from voting more than once, even though nearly every expert agrees that such "voter fraud" almost never happens.

Thus it's not obvious why voter lists would need to be so enthusiastically "cleaned" in the first place.

Between 2016 and 2018, more than seventeen million Americans had their names removed from voting lists across the country. How many of these people later tried—and failed—to exercise their right to vote? One estimate puts the number at over a million.

"It's kind of mind-blowing," Baiye reflected. "You're basically saying if I don't use my right, you'll take my right away. That's utterly ridiculous."

On top of voter purges, opponents of people power have launched a new campaign to stop even more people from voting—ironically, under the guise of "protecting" elections.

Around the year 2000, Republican politicians in states throughout the country began passing laws that require identification, usually a driver's license, in order to vote. Thirty-four states now have voter ID requirements, a totally new development in the history of voting in America.

When Texas added a strict voter ID law to its books, eighty-three-year-old Floyd Carrier quickly learned what the law's authors had in mind. Carrier showed up to vote in 2016 with his veteran's card, an expired driver's license, and his voter registration card. He'd been voting legally for decades. Now, however—without a new license—the poll worker turned Carrier away.

Voter ID laws are supposed to reduce the chance of so-called voter fraud, which happens when someone votes illegally (such as voting more than once). Critics of the laws, on the other hand, point to research that shows actual voter fraud almost *never* occurs in America. (In Ohio, for example, a state that recently passed very strict voter ID laws, state officials found only twenty-seven votes that were *possibly* fraudulent in the 2020 presidential election— or a tiny 0.0005 percent of the total votes cast.)

We need ID cards to drive, fly on an airplane, and in some places even to go to school. How could requiring a voter to show identification be a form of discrimination or a rule meant to suppress, rather than protect, voting in America?

Over twenty million Americans—nearly 10 percent of the voting-age population—do not have official identification cards such as a driver's license or passport. The majority of these people are poor. Many—like Floyd Carrier—are elderly, born at a time, or in a place, when getting a birth certificate was not as common as it is today. A large percentage of them are African American, and an even larger percentage are Native American. Getting the documents to qualify for a driver's license, and then securing the license itself, can be expensive. For financial reasons as well, voter ID laws function the way poll taxes did under Jim Crow, making it hard or even impossible for some people to vote because they cannot afford the cost.

The people most affected by new voter ID laws are some of the least powerful in the United States, people for whom voting may well be the only, or the best, way for them to make their voices heard.

The opponents of people power have pushed back on the gains of the Civil Rights Movement with an arsenal of new weapons for tamping down on voting rights.

And in recent years, they have found a surprising ally: the Supreme Court.

The Voting Rights Act gives the federal government the power to review any changes to voting laws in states with a history of discrimination.

Maggie Bozeman understood why oversight was so desperately needed in her corner of Alabama. But many miles away, Supreme Court justices in Washington, DC, seemed increasingly (or willingly) blind to the attacks on voting rights all over the South.

In 2013, in a case called *Shelby County v. Holder*, the court decided that the federal government no longer had any reason to review changes to voting-rights decisions made by states—the preclearance required by the Voting Rights Act. The greatest accomplishment of people-power activists, the Voting Rights Act, was now being gutted, some said, by the very court that was supposed to be upholding all Americans' civil rights.

For nearly 250 years, American people had fought for an unshakable constitutional right to vote—one that could not be taken away. *Shelby County v. Holder* threatened to undo all of that.

In her famous dissent from the majority's opinion— which, in a gutsy act of protest, she presented out loud in court—Justice Ruth Bader Ginsburg declared that "throwing out preclearance when it has worked and is continuing to work to stop discriminatory changes is like throwing away your umbrella in a rainstorm because you are not getting wet."

In the ten years and more since *Shelby County v. Holder*, the forces of American democracy have been tossed about by stormy weather. But over two hundred years of fighting have taught ordinary people to button up, show up, and be counted.

THE GERRY-MANDER.

sons

"The Gerry-Mander. A new species of *Monster*, which appeared in
Essex South District in Jan. 1812." (Original caption.)

MASSACHUSETTS HISTORICAL SOCIETY

Chapter Fifteen

DIVISIONS

Fort Bend County had changed a lot in forty years. The place where Willie Velásquez and SVREP won their first voter registration victory still had a large Mexican American population in 2021, but its fastest-growing community was Asian American. Thousands of immigrants from Vietnam, Korea, the Pacific Islands, and India had made new homes for themselves in this sprawling area near the city of Houston.

But Texas's large and growing Asian American population has little or no representation in the state's government. Hyunja Norman, a Korean American community leader, commented that "it's like [lawmakers] don't even know we are here."

In 2021, when millions of people were left without power during a record freeze, the county sent out emergency alerts—in English—but many people could not understand them and get the help they needed. And during the Covid-19 pandemic, when Fort Bend's Asian American residents became the target of racist, anti-Asian attacks and hate crimes, their own House representative, a white man, refused to condemn what was happening.

"Who is going to stand up for our community?" Norman asked.

Norman and her community voted in every election. So how could they lack representation in a country based on the principle of "one person, one vote"?

Kathay Feng has pinpointed the cause of the problem. Feng is a voting-rights activist who has led fights for free and fair elections all across the United States. She works for Common Cause, an organization whose mission is to make sure that our government is "truly of, by, and for the people."

Feng has spent her entire career trying to make sure that all Americans have an equal right to vote and that communities in places like Fort Bend are represented in a meaningful way. She is inspired, in part, by her experiences of exclusion as an Asian American girl in Texas and by scenes she witnessed early in her career. Feng remembers elderly Asian American voters who were turned away "because poll workers could not read their names."

Feng has seen firsthand all the obstacles voters face

when trying to make their voices heard. But the thing she worries about most is a problem that most people *can't* see: a practice known as "gerrymandering."

Feng calls gerrymandering "the toxic lead pipes that poison our democracy": It's the reason that places like Fort Bend, and other communities all over the country, cannot make their voices heard.

And it's no accident.

To understand gerrymandering, you have to understand how votes are counted in American elections.

Today, each state legislature (that is, elected representatives who make the laws in each state) is responsible for creating congressional voting districts of equal population. Every representative from these districts, in turn, casts a vote in the House of Representatives to reflect the interests of that district's voters. (Each state is also represented by two US senators, who are elected in statewide votes every six years.)

There are now 435 representatives in Congress, representing 435 voting (or electoral) districts of equal size. From the earliest days of the United States, however, some politicians realized that they could draw district boundaries to give one party or group better representation than another. Fiddling with the boundaries of voting districts to affect election outcomes became known as gerrymandering because of the notorious efforts of Governor Elbridge Gerry of Massachusetts. Gerry helped create a new district around the city of Boston that gave greater power to voters in his party, the Jeffersonian Republicans.

In 1812, a political cartoonist drew what he called "The Gerry-Mander, A new species of *Monster*, which appeared in *Essex South District*"—an image combining the governor's name with a salamander.

The name, and the image, stuck. The practice of twisting and distorting district lines, often to a ridiculous extent, became part of our political history.

At times, gerrymandering was used simply to give one party an advantage over the other—since winning elections, after all, was the goal of political parties in the first place.

But other, more sinister motives crept into gerrymandering, too.

In the South, gerrymandering was deliberately used to dilute the influence of even those few Black people who could vote, through a strategy called "cracking and stacking." "Cracking" was the practice of drawing district lines to break up a single community of African American voters. Each member of the local electorate could still vote, but the collective impact of their votes was weakened, if not outright eliminated. "Stacking" was the practice of adding more white voters to a district by stretching a district line to loop in a white neighborhood, artificially creating a white majority of voters.

In Fort Bend County, the state legislature has drawn district lines to crack the Asian American community into smaller pieces. Each small piece is part of a larger district with a white majority. No single district includes a large number of Asian American voters, and as a result, their representation in the government has been weakened.

The two-hundred-plus-year-old story of gerrymandering took an ominous turn after the election of Barack Obama, a Democrat, as president in 2008. That year, the Republican Party suffered staggering losses—including both the presidency and control of Congress, with some people suggesting that the party could fade into obscurity for a generation or more. Obama entered the White House as one of the most popular new presidents in history, and with the Democratic Party controlling both the House of Representatives and the Senate, he seemed unstoppable.

But a few people in the Republican Party saw opportunity in defeat.

Under US election law, state legislatures are able to redraw the boundaries of their House electoral districts *every ten years*—based on the results of the United States Census, which conducts a new count of the American population once every decade. The law was written to make sure that changes in the population are fairly reflected in the electoral map.

Fairness, however, has rarely been factored into the process. Whoever is in power in each state at the time gets to draw the lines—a huge opportunity for the party that happens to hold the majority. After Obama's election, the Republican Party decided to focus on a handful of state legislature elections, with the goal of winning a majority of seats in key states. That way, Republicans would be in a position to shape election districts to their advantage.

In 2010, the plan worked exactly as the Republicans had hoped. Soon after, in key states all over the country, teams of Republican map drawers got to work.

Gerrymandering has always depended on cleverness to draw district lines so that the people who support your party are inside them. Understanding who lives in a given district, and how they might vote, is the key to success.

But in recent years, technology has supercharged politicians' ability to know precisely who lives where, what they like and don't like, and who they are most likely to vote for.

By using a sophisticated computer software called

Maptitude, state officials are able to find out almost everything about the people who live in a given area. They then
plug in this data to draw new political maps—making sure
to *include* inside the lines the people who will vote for their
party, and to *exclude* those who won't. These maps are reliable guides to how voters will cast their ballots in a future
election. Technology takes out the guesswork and replaces
it with up-to-date information. The result? A party in
power at the right time—that is, the party that gets to
draw the maps—wins more elections. And that's exactly
what happened to the Republicans after 2010.

How much of a difference can a new electoral map
make? Consider these numbers from Pennsylvania.

In the 2006 election for the US House of Representatives, Democrats received 2,229,091 votes overall,
and Republicans received 1,732,163. Across the state as
a whole, Democrats received 496,928 *more* votes than
Republicans. As one would expect, more votes resulted in
more Democratic representatives heading to Congress in
2007 (eleven Democrats versus eight Republicans).

Then in 2010, Republicans gained control of the state
legislature and redrew the state's congressional district maps.

In 2012, the first House of Representatives election
after the gerrymander, Democratic candidates received
2,793,538 votes overall, and Republican candidates received

2,710,070. Democrats had still received a majority of votes in the state, though by a much smaller margin of 83,468. But the gerrymander worked its magic: Since the Democrats in Pennsylvania won a majority of the votes cast for House seats, that would mean that Democrats won a majority of those seats, right? Exactly the opposite happened. Because of the way the new district lines were drawn, despite winning fewer votes than Democrats in Pennsylvania, Republican candidates won *thirteen* of the state's House seats, and Democrats only *five* (the remaining seat went to an independent candidate).

The new technology had neutralized Pennsylvania's Democratic (and democratic) majority.

In the United States as a whole that year, 1.4 million more people voted for Democrats over Republicans in House races, but Republicans *still* won the chamber by an overwhelming majority—thirty-three seats.

And it wasn't just a defeat for the Democratic Party. Gerrymandering made sure that the policies that a majority of Americans had voted for, like gun control, would not become law.

Norman Ornstein, an expert at the conservative American Enterprise Institute, had this to say about recent election results: "It means basically that the whole constitutional notion of the House as a mirror of popular views comes into jeopardy."

Without gerrymandering, these election results would have been much less lopsided. Politicians would have been forced to compete more against one another while persuading undecided voters to support them—instead of simply relying on maps to do all the work. Ideas and opinions, more than maps, would influence election results. Voters' wishes would be heard.

Extreme gerrymandering has made the country less democratic, and less responsive to people power. Gerrymandering is *designed* to make individual votes matter less and geography matter more.

Gerrymandering could lead to a dystopia where finely tuned voting maps take away our power as voters to have our unique voices heard in Washington. It's not clear which side will win—people power or gerrymandering. But people like Kathay Feng are fighting to make sure that real democracy wins out. "Everything hangs in the balance with the future of fair redistricting," she says.

In Texas, local people are pushing back hard against efforts to divide and weaken their communities. A voting-rights activist named Ashley Cheng says, "We are in a time of history where we're really rising up as a community and making sure that our political voices are heard.... We have so much in common in a need for representation."

Protesters gather outside the Supreme Court on the day of the
Citizens United decision. January 15, 2015.

Chapter Sixteen

BIG MONEY, BIG PROBLEMS

IN 2009, A REPUBLICAN CONGRESSMAN FROM SOUTH Carolina named Bob Inglis proposed a bill to tax carbon emissions. With rising global temperatures on many Americans' minds, it seemed like a good idea. Climate change was already threatening American communities through rising sea levels, especially in states with long coastlines, like South Carolina. By taxing the main thing that contributed to global warming (the carbon that results from the burning of fossil fuels), Inglis hoped to slow the damage being done to the planet—and to his constituents. In short, he was doing a good job representing the people who had voted for him.

A short time later, Inglis ran into trouble. Donations to his reelection campaign dried up. Groups of protesters started showing up wherever he spoke, shouting so loudly that he couldn't be heard over the clamor. His opponent during his next reelection campaign, Trey Gowdy, started gaining ground and attracting more donations.

In June 2010, Inglis lost his seat in a Republican Party primary election to Gowdy, and quit Congress for good at the end of his term.

Two years earlier, an organization called Americans for Prosperity had circulated a "carbon pledge," which stated that the government should never seek to control carbon emissions. Mike Pence, a congressman from Indiana, signed the pledge, as did many other Republicans seeking reelection in 2010. Campaign donations flowed in, and all of them won.

Was this a coincidence?

It turns out that Americans for Prosperity got its support from two billionaire brothers whose company, Koch Industries, makes its money from oil and gas, the very products that contribute to global warming and that Inglis and many others in government were trying to regulate. Each year, Americans for Prosperity spends millions of dollars supporting candidates who block efforts to reduce carbon emissions. The group has also been the main force behind a propaganda campaign to cast doubt on the idea that climate change is happening at all.

Groups like Americans for Prosperity have sprung up across the United States, spending billions of dollars to broadcast some ideas and to shout down others—all to make sure that their wishes are respected in Congress, statehouses, and city halls. The candidates they fund can easily outspend their opponents—covering more ground, spending more on advertisements, and getting more attention for their campaigns. The noise they make is drowning out the voices of ordinary Americans.

Just as someone who has lots of money can afford a bigger house and a fancier car, money in politics has a way of making some people's wishes come true at the expense of others'. For that reason, some Americans have fought back against how money influences our democracy.

If we want real democracy, the thinking goes, we have to *regulate* how much private money can be placed in the palms of political candidates and elected officials. Otherwise, political equality—the principle of "one person, one vote"—will be trumped by political donations.

At different times, different laws have been passed to control the flow of money into American politics or at least to act as a check on its influence.

One of the most important election laws limits the amount of money any one person can give to a political candidate. Under the Federal Election Campaign Act, each citizen can donate a maximum of $3,300 to a single political candidate during one election cycle. Other laws, at both national and state levels, require politicians to disclose who donated to them, and how much, as a way of letting the public know *who* is trying to influence American politics and what their agendas might be.

It was never a foolproof system, and there were always hidden gaps where money flowed freely through. But until 2010, Americans seemed to agree that we need a dam to block the power of money from swamping the power of the people.

All that changed when one fateful Supreme Court decision took a wrecking ball to the dam.

In 2008, an organization named Citizens United planned on broadcasting a film that criticized Hillary Clinton, a candidate for president, during the presidential primary. With lots of corporate money at its disposal, the group planned to pay to have the film shown on cable television all over the country. Before that could happen, however, the Federal Election Commission, a government agency, blocked the film because it would have violated a federal law banning corporations, labor unions, or other nonprofit groups from independent political spending—spending meant to influence voters—in the run-up to elections.

The law had been put in place to curb the influence of powerful, wealthy organizations on the American political process.

Citizens United wasn't happy about the government telling it what it could do with its film. So it filed a lawsuit against the Federal Election Commission, and it eventually made its way to the US Supreme Court.

In 2010, the influence of money, especially big money, on American politics was not news. For one thing, running for office, in the era of television and political advertising, had gotten very expensive. Political campaigns need a constant flow of cash to pay for the staff and the media coverage that help candidates get elected. While a few politicians accept only small donations from ordinary people—or accept public funds established by local, state, or federal programs—most candidates have been happy to take whatever help they can get. In fact, running for office without a big account, or wealthy donors, can seem all but impossible: It's no accident, some experts argue, that so many members of Congress are millionaires.

Even before the landmark Supreme Court decision, money spoke very loudly in American politics. But *Citizens United v. Federal Election Commission* turned that volume all the way up.

The court decided that telling organizations they

could not spend money to support political candidates was a violation of the First Amendment, which protects Americans' right to free speech ("Congress shall make no law... abridging the freedom of speech"). But to arrive at that decision, it also came up with two novel arguments: first, that spending money is a form of speech (and therefore covered by the First Amendment), and second, that corporations, labor unions, or nonprofit organizations have the same rights as individual citizens.

Following the *Citizens United* decision, wealthy donors, corporations, and organizations of many different political stripes immediately got to work. In the years since then, they have spent *billions* of dollars trying to influence voters and elections.

The new flow of money into politics is sometimes called "dark money" because the source of the dollars is hidden. Dark-money groups can accept donations from anyone interested in their work, and they do not have to reveal who those people (or companies) are. Dark money makes a mockery of the laws meant to establish spending limits by groups and individuals.

To make matters even more mysterious, sometimes dark-money groups donate to super PACs (political action committees), organizations that can spend millions of dollars helping a candidate get elected. The identity of the people donating to super PACs remains entirely hidden.

Why does this new tidal wave of dark money matter?

In addition to helping elect candidates, dark-money groups can influence

- how laws get written;
- how laws get enforced;
- how the public thinks about important issues, such as climate change, health care, and education—including through deliberate misinformation campaigns involving outright lies.

And because so much of their work is behind the scenes, the influence of dark-money groups can be difficult to detect.

With so much money flooding the American political system, every elected official feels the pressure to raise more and more of it, just to keep up with their opponents. Today, the amount of money a candidate raises almost *always* determines who wins and who loses.

Candidates spend hours every day calling donors

(especially wealthy donors) to contribute to their reelection campaigns. Senator Alan K. Simpson of Wyoming described the process bluntly: "You get a Rolodex; you go outside the building for a whole day and dial numbers of jerks you've never heard of in your whole life to get money out of 'em."

With a direct line to politicians, people with money and power have a much better chance than ordinary voters of making their needs and interests heard.

Because they face reelection every two years, members of the House of Representatives can be trapped in what seems like a never-ending cycle of fundraising. The former House Republican leader Robert Michel once reported having to attend five fundraising events *every night*.

Another congressman pointed to the *Citizens United* decision as the culprit. "If you want your voice to be heard as opposed to some outside group speaking for you," Republican Reid Ribble of Wisconsin complained, "you better do your job and raise enough money that you can."

Senator Sheldon Whitehouse, a Democrat from Rhode Island, is one of the nation's leading critics of dark money in American politics. He even wrote a book on the subject entitled *Captured: The Corporate Infiltration of American Democracy*. "If there's a person in the Senate who the...big dark money crowd is more annoyed with than me, I don't know who that person is," he said. "So I viewed myself as being very high up that target list." But Whitehouse was not immune to the need to raise millions of dollars to counter his opponents, especially given his vocal opposition to dark money.

All of this time spent focusing on money has a direct impact on how our elected officials do their jobs. The hours they spend fundraising take away from the time political leaders have to spend on the very things they were elected to do: listen to the people who voted for them and solve the problems we elected them to fix in the first place.

Anonymous forces shaping how our laws get made. Politicians spending most of their time calling or rubbing elbows with wealthy donors. Well-funded organizations spreading ideas that influence how people vote. This is what happens when our elections drown in dark money.

Since *Citizens United*, the voices of ordinary people have increasingly been muted.

According to one expert, "the decision has helped reinforce the growing sense that our democracy primarily serves the interests of the wealthy few, and that democratic participation for the vast majority of citizens is of relatively little value."

And given how elites have always felt about people power, maybe that's not a side effect of all the money being spent. Maybe that was the product they were trying to buy all along.

Rioters crashing through the doors of the US Capitol in an attempt to overturn the results of the 2020 election. January 6, 2021.

WIN MCNAMEE, GETTY IMAGES

Chapter Seventeen

TRUTH AND LIES

IN SEPTEMBER 2020, A MAN POSTED PHOTOGRAPHS ON his social media account of a large number of mail-in ballots piled in a dumpster in Sonoma, California. His post suggested a possible attempt to hide or destroy the votes of thousands of Californians, calling the discovery "shocking" and "big if true." The story was retweeted tens of thousands of times and quickly attracted national attention.

A little over a month later, on Election Day 2020, a local journalist in Chicago tweeted a story about election workers supposedly handing out Sharpie pens to voters to fill out their ballots. These pens made large ink blots on the ballots, she claimed, and caused them to be rejected. Her post included an image of one of these ballots with a vote for Donald Trump. All day on November 7, and for weeks afterward, the story of Sharpie-blotted ballots appeared and reappeared all over the country as it ballooned into a scandal. One tweet read

They gave Trump voters sharpies and now their votes are being invalidated! WTF!

Shortly after the 2020 election, rumors began circulating online that thousands of votes for President-elect Joseph Biden had been cast illegally by Democratic women who had "stolen" the maiden names of Republican women voters.

In 2020, some newspapers, politicians, and television anchors were making it seem that voter fraud was everywhere. They told a frightening story of American democracy under attack by tricksters trying to cast votes illegally.

There was just one problem: Absolutely none of it was true.

If there was no voter fraud to begin with, then why were so many people acting as if it were real?

It turns out that voter fraud is a myth that is almost as old as the United States of America.

- In 1807, male voters in New Jersey accused women of voter fraud, and used it as an excuse to take away their voting rights.
- During Reconstruction, newly enfranchised Black voters were accused of voter fraud even though, as historians have shown, it was white supremacists who routinely stuffed ballot boxes with fake votes.
- Later in the century, voter-fraud accusations helped to cut back immigrants' ability to vote.

Throughout history, the myth has reappeared wherever some people have tried to shrink our democracy by making it harder for other people, usually women or people of color, to vote.

In recent years, the myth of voter fraud has reappeared once again. Why now?

Some experts have argued that the shift in America's population toward, eventually, a nonwhite majority has revived old fears of too much democracy in a country where white people held so much political power for so long.

Others have shown that by shrinking our democracy, government no longer has to be responsive to ordinary people's needs. Fewer government services (such as schools, roads, or health care) means lower taxes, particularly for wealthy people. By weakening people power, some people can increase their private economic power.

Because of the accomplishments of people-power activists over the past 150 years, it is no longer possible to simply *take away* some people's votes as the night riders did at the end of Reconstruction.

But the voter-fraud myth acts as a smoke screen for doing just that. By seeking to deny the real outcome of elections, a new generation of politicians and people-power enemies are trying to erase the wishes of millions of American voters.

The voter-fraud trick works like this:

- Claim that your opponent has been unfairly elected by fraudulent voting.
- Deny the fairness or legitimacy of an election outcome, even if all the evidence shows that it was fair and properly conducted.
- Declare that you are the rightly elected candidate, even though the evidence shows you didn't win.

♦ Create a cloud of suspicion and doubt, aided by your supporters in the media.

Candidates who refuse to accept the fairly decided outcome of a vote are called "election deniers" because they choose to tell lies about what really happened. It may seem harmless: After all, being a sore loser has never been against the law.

But in the past several years, lying has changed from a dirty trick to something much more sinister.

In a world where lies can spread like wildfire over the internet and social media, where it can be difficult to sort fact from fiction, election deniers have succeeded in casting doubt on our entire system of voting and democracy.

Larry Jacobs, an expert on American politics, described the new political lying as "a disease that is spreading through our political process," adding that "this is about the entire electoral system and what constitutes legitimate elections. All of that is now up in the air."

After the presidential election of 2020, Joseph Biden was declared the winner.

His opponent, former president Donald Trump, refused to accept the outcome of the election and cried foul.

Trump had spent four years as president insulting the nation's immigrants, opposing the new movement for racial justice, and blocking every attempt to expand voting rights. He elevated political lying to new heights, with claims about everything from climate change to the Covid-19 epidemic that contradicted science and factual evidence. Now that his presidency had gone down in defeat, he took his falsehoods to a new level.

The Trump campaign filed lawsuits across the nation, seeking to challenge the vote count in different states. The courts decided that the election had been fair and the votes counted accurately. Even his own attorney general, William Barr, concluded that the election results were valid. In short, no evidence ever emerged of significant voter fraud in the 2020 presidential election.

But Trump, who still occupied the White House as the outgoing president, refused to give up. He and his supporters continued to spread false information about voter fraud despite the fact that Joseph Biden had won a clear majority of both individual votes and votes in the Electoral College.

Lying about winning the election was only part of Trump's plan. The president and a group of conspirators also tried to throw a wrench into the election machinery, especially in the state of Georgia.

Trump's allies reached out to a group of Republican officials in Georgia and persuaded them to present themselves at the Georgia statehouse on December 14, 2020, as the rightful slate of electors, who would then vote for Donald Trump in the Electoral College. (The *actual* electors were meeting that day, to cast their votes for the winner of the popular vote, Joseph Biden.)

This "fake electors" plan quickly fell apart when several of the officials refused to go ahead with it, fearing that it was illegal.

In a related scheme, Trump himself placed a phone call on January 2, 2021, to Georgia Secretary of State Brad Raffensperger, whose job included overseeing all elections in the state. During that call, the president asked Raffensperger to "find" more votes—enough to make sure that the president had received the majority of votes there. In fact, Trump had lost Georgia by nearly twelve thousand votes—and Raffensperger refused the president's request.

All the while, Trump and his allies repeated their claims that the election results were tainted.

Almost three years later, Trump faced both federal and state charges for illegal efforts to overturn the 2020 election results. In these cases, government officials viewed Trump's efforts as a criminal attempt to undermine the will of the people who had voted in the 2020 election.

As 2020 came to an end, Trump's complaints about the supposedly rigged election grew louder and louder. By the new year, in the last days of Trump's presidency, his cries of election fraud reached a climax.

On January 6, 2021, the day when Congress was meeting to certify, or officially approve, the outcome of the 2020 election, President Trump gave a fiery speech outside the White House to a large group of his supporters.

"And we fight," he exclaimed, using words that echoed the Red Shirts and other white supremacists who fought to destroy democracy in the South after Reconstruction. "We fight like hell. And if you don't fight like hell, you're not going to have a country anymore."

Joined by thousands of other protesters, the crowd marched down the National Mall to the US Capitol. And when they reached the doors, they took their cue from the president.

Rioters attacked police officers and crashed through windows and doors in an attempt to reach the chambers where the House and Senate were meeting. Some of them threatened to kill members of Congress; others aimed to hang Vice President Pence, who was on Capitol Hill that morning in his role as president of the Senate, to preside over the election certification. For the first time since the War of 1812, the seat of American democracy had come under siege—but this time, instead of the British Army, it was Trump's supporters who tried to overthrow the will of the American people.

The attackers had a range of motives. Some may simply have not wanted Joseph Biden to be president—whatever the cost to our democracy. Others, however, had taken the lies of President Trump and his supporters (including many in Congress and in the media) at face value, and may well have believed that they were "saving democracy" from a fraudulent election.

The members of Congress who were trapped inside the building—where they had arrived that morning to perform their duties under the United States Constitution—recalled moments of genuine fear and terror as the attack on democracy unfolded.

"We were told to pull out our gas masks, which many of us had never seen, never knew how to use, and then we were told to get down onto the floor," recalled Representative Pramila Jayapal of Washington.

"There was a very real fear that these people who were pounding on the doors, maybe just 15 feet from us, were going to get in and that we would not make it out," she said.

Only after many hours were law enforcement officers able to push the rioters back.

Over months of questioning and exhaustive research, what became known as the January 6 committee uncovered a terrifying conspiracy against the institutions of American democracy, coordinated by some of the most powerful people in the United States.

The voter-fraud myth made this conspiracy possible.

"Beginning election night and continuing through Jan. 6 and thereafter," the committee found, "Donald Trump...disseminated false allegations of fraud related to the 2020 presidential election...and for purposes of soliciting contributions. These false claims provoked his supporters to violence on Jan. 6."

Deliberate political lies led to real political violence. For the first time in our history, opponents of democracy tried to block the peaceful transfer of power from one president to the next.

There is a direct and jarring historical parallel between the violence of January 6, 2021, and "Redemption," when white supremacists sought to put an end to Reconstruction. When insurrectionists on January 6 paraded the Confederate flag in the US Capitol, arguably the most sacred ground in America, there was little doubt about the racist undertones of rioters inspired by Trump and egged on by other white conservative politicians. In both cases, some people resorted to mob violence when they couldn't achieve their goals through a free and fair election.

The sight of the Capitol being protected by the police, many of them Black, was a reminder that Black citizens have always stood up for freedom and democracy in a nation that denied them the loyalty they showed. On January 6, Black people helped shield a legally conducted election even as Black voting rights were under attack. Without their efforts, we may well have lost our democracy in an angry insurrection.

In the end, the institutions of American government withstood the attack by Trump and his allies on January 6, and Biden was sworn in as president two weeks later. However, the years since have revealed how damaging, and infectious, political lying can be.

Some Republican leaders condemned the attacks. Mitch McConnell, the Republican leader of the Senate and an ally of President Trump, had this to say about January 6, which he witnessed firsthand: "It was a violent insurrection for the purpose of trying to prevent the peaceful transfer of power after a legitimately certified election from one administration to the next."

But many more elected officials and candidates for office *continued* to repeat election-fraud lies as the 2024 election approached. They sensed a political advantage in arguing that Donald Trump had actually won the election, even though no evidence ever emerged to support that claim. As a result, and thanks to news organizations willing to broadcast these political lies, large percentages of voters became persuaded that the 2020 presidential election was "stolen."

Lying has become the latest tool for chipping away at people power. It is the opposite of voting power because it undercuts the American people's wishes.

Where does this leave our democracy?

Congressman Jamie Raskin of Maryland was in the Capitol on January 6 when the attackers broke in. Raskin's family had joined him in the building that day as a show of support; his son Tommy's funeral had taken place only the day before, the saddest day of their lives, according to Raskin. Worried about the protests, they asked the congressman if they would be safe in his office.

"I told them—of course it should be safe," Raskin recalled. "This is the Capitol."

Raskin's family spent the next several hours barricaded in an office, hiding under a desk. They sent desperate text messages. They thought they were going to die.

Jamie Raskin has spent the years since doing everything in his power to investigate the January 6 attack on democracy and to bring its perpetrators to justice. He blames that day, as well as the nation's sharply divided political situation, on election lies. "There's a difference between fact and fiction," Raskin says, adding, "there's a difference between truth and lies and conspiracy theories.

"And the struggle to defend democratic institutions," Raskin concludes, "is interwoven with the struggle to arrive at the truth and to tell the truth to the people."

In 2023, the simple power of truth telling has begun to rescue our fragile system of government. It's a power all of us have, including you: to make judgments about what is true and what is false, and about whom we can trust to represent us.

Alabama state police prepare to attack peaceful voting-rights demonstrators who have just crossed the Edmund Pettus Bridge on March 7, 1965. John Lewis is pictured on the right, wearing a tan raincoat.

Epilogue

MORE IS MORE

ON MARCH 7, 1965, AS JOHN LEWIS CROSSED OVER THE Edmund Pettus Bridge in a protest for voting rights, hundreds of Alabama state policemen charged into the marchers in a violent assault.

Lewis suffered a skull fracture when a state trooper struck his head with a baton; he carried scars on his head for the rest of his life. It was neither the first nor the last time he risked death for democracy.

Many years later, John Lewis ran for Congress and won. Over a long career representing the people of Georgia, John Lewis remained one of America's most passionate and committed defenders of voting rights for all Americans.

A year after John Lewis's death in July of 2020, the US House of Representatives passed the John R. Lewis Voting Rights Advancement Act of 2021.

The bill strengthens the provisions of the Voting Rights

Act and seeks to sweep away all the anti-voter restrictions of recent years, making it easier and safer for all Americans of voting age to cast a ballot. It injects strength into the federal government's ability to make sure that every citizen, in every state, can vote freely.

For many, the act represents America's best chance for reviving our democracy at a time when voting rights have come under attack. One of the act's strongest supporters in the Senate, Raphael Warnock, commented that "Voting rights is not just some other issue alongside other rights. It's the very framework in which we get to fight for all the things we care about."

Despite its many supporters, opponents of people power blocked the John R. Lewis Voting Rights Advancement Act in the Senate, where it failed to pass. But they did not block the movement for change that lay behind it—and that movement is growing, day by day, as new people step in and join the fight.

The unfinished work of people power in America is passing to a new generation of voters and soon-to-be voters. John Lewis, like so many freedom fighters before him, joined the fight as a teenager. It will be people like him—and like you—with hopes and wishes of their own, who finally ensure that our country makes good on the promises of democracy.

EPILOGUE

The Founding Fathers created a brilliant blueprint for democracy, but one thing most of them agreed on is that the people couldn't be trusted with it.

It was the people themselves who had to force the country to become a genuine democracy—and it took them more than two hundred years to do it. In fighting these fights, democracy's heroes showed us why more, not less, democracy is the American way.

More democracy means more equality.

More democracy means more justice.

More democracy means more freedom.

How do we get more democracy? You may believe that more democracy is out of reach. In those moments, we encourage you to think about Robert Smalls, Mabel Ping-Hua Lee, Zitkála-Šá, and Fannie Lou Hamer. By going after the vote, these Americans turned powerlessness into power at times of great peril, and at great risk to themselves. And they won.

Unlikely people, people on the outside, are often the ones most likely to see the right path forward, because they understand what holds us back.

All of them had voices and wishes for a different future. All of them took a vow to make our democracy bigger and better. All of them acted on that vow and made more of our democracy.

Today, the threats to our democracy are as dire as ever, but the lesson of the story we have told in *Represent* is that change is possible, one brave person at a time.

ACKNOWLEDGMENTS

As always, we thank the fearless Tanya McKinnon, our agent, for her dedication to our work. Our wonderful editor, Lisa Yoskowitz, keeps us on a steady course; we are so grateful for her efforts, and for the support of her colleagues Lily Choi, Alexandra Houdeshell, Jen Graham, Gabrielle Chang, Karina Granda, Patricia Alvarado, Bill Grace, Andie Divelbiss, Savannah Kennelly, Sadie Trombetta, Victoria Stapleton, Christie Michel, David Koral, Sherri Schmidt, Rick Ball, and everyone else at Little, Brown Books for Young Readers who helped bring this book into the world.

Marc celebrated thirty years of marriage to his wife, Patty, as this manuscript was wrapping up. This book, like everything else, is part of their journey together.

As this book came to life, Michael wished his mother, Addie Mae Dyson—a brilliant woman who couldn't vote

ACKNOWLEDGMENTS

for nearly the first thirty years of her life—a happy eighty-seventh birthday.

Lastly, we wish to acknowledge the teachers, librarians, and others who fight for the free circulation of books in our embattled democracy.

PEOPLE-POWER IDEAS

TODAY'S PEOPLE-POWER HEROES HAVE A NEW SET OF IDEAS for how to get more democracy.

In the following section, we describe some of them. Which ones will you fight for?

GETTING RID OF THE ELECTORAL COLLEGE

The framers of the Constitution created the Electoral College to block the will of the people.

In two recent elections, the Electoral College handed the presidency to candidates who *did not win the popular vote*. In the most extreme case, Donald Trump became president despite the fact that Hillary Clinton had won three million more votes than he did. (Because of the winner-take-all system in how most states allocate their electoral votes, Trump won more electoral votes than Clinton.)

To many people, it now seems like the relic of a distant past. In the present, it still plays that same role; it has become so problematic in recent years that one expert calls it "a ticking time bomb." According to a recent poll, 65 percent of voting-age adults in America think the Electoral College should be abolished, and many experts and voting-rights groups are calling for a constitutional amendment to get rid of it.

Abolishing the Electoral College would finally remove one of the major roadblocks to real democracy.

EXPANDING THE HOUSE OF REPRESENTATIVES

According to the Constitution, there should be one representative for every thirty thousand citizens. If this were still true today, the House of Representatives, because of population growth, would have to add more than ten thousand representatives. Today, the total number of House members is capped by law at 435.

Congress has the power to change the number of House members, and it has made changes to this number at different points in American history. Increasing the size of the House (some people estimate that fifty new members would be the ideal number, given the space available on Capitol Hill) would mean more representation, and more points of view reflected in Congress.

MAKE VOTING EASIER, NOT HARDER

Because actual voter fraud is so rare in America, many activists and politicians are fighting for changes in our voting system that would make it easier to vote:

- expanding the use of mail-in ballots so that people who have difficulty traveling to the polls can get their votes in
- making voter registration easier, such as by allowing same-day registration for all voters
- allowing early voting, rather than limiting it to a single day
- providing translation services for non-English speakers

Some states allow these now, but many are moving in the opposite direction, making voting harder, instead of easier.

RANKED-CHOICE VOTING

In most cases, when we vote, we choose one candidate. But in elections where there are three or more candidates for office, the person who receives the most votes and wins the election could still receive less than a *majority* of votes, which is sometimes called a *plurality* of votes. A winner, therefore, may not represent the wishes of most voters.

A new voting system called ranked-choice voting seeks to fix that problem, making voting itself more democratic and more reflective of what the voters actually want. In ranked-choice voting, voters rank their choices in order of preference—first, second, third, and so on—rather than selecting a single winner. If no "first choice" candidate wins a majority of votes, the system turns to voters' second, third, or fourth choices and factors them in until one candidate wins a majority.

The state of Maine uses ranked-choice voting in its elections, as do many major cities.

Ranked-choice voting ensures that winning candidates represent the largest number of voters. If you vote under a ranked-choice system, it is more likely that a winning candidate reflects your wishes.

CHANGING FELON DISFRANCHISEMENT LAWS

Seventeen states now give back voting rights to citizens after they have been released from prison. Maine and Vermont allow citizens to vote even when they are incarcerated.

If every state restored voting rights to former prisoners, over a million more people—people who have already paid their debt to society—would be allowed to vote.

MAKE VOTING MANDATORY

We require all people to attend school, pay taxes, and obey traffic laws. But the one action that makes democracy possible—voting—is completely optional.

Some prodemocracy advocates, however, argue that we should all be required to vote, a rule referred to as "universal civil participation," or informally as "100 percent democracy." In Australia, where voting is mandatory, a whopping 92 percent of eligible voters turn out for elections.

A democracy activist named Miles Rapoport argues that "one of the ways in which to get the consent of all the governed is to make sure that everyone, every citizen, is voting as a matter of civic obligation. And interestingly, we do this now for jury duty. Everyone has to serve on a jury if you are called. And we don't think of that as an imposition. So, we think that that same logic should extend to the area of voting."

GET RID OF PARTISAN GERRYMANDERING

As it turns out, computer programs such as Maptitude can be used to create neutral election maps as well as maps tilted in favor of one party. Guided by bipartisan citizens' groups, programmers can draw lines that capture the unique diversity of America's population instead of sharpening the dividing lines between our two major political parties. A number of states, including California, Colorado, Michigan, and North Carolina, have done exactly this.

As district maps become fairer, they will better represent the views of all a state's voters instead of artificially dividing them into opposing political camps or giving one party an unfair advantage over another. Politics would become more competitive because it would be more difficult for a single party to win elections. Moreover, many experts argue, if voters believe that the system represents them fairly, more people will participate in elections.

LIMIT THE INFLUENCE OF MONEY IN POLITICS

A number of elected officials have bravely put forward legislation meant to control the flow of money into politics—by limiting campaign contributions, by making all information about contributions publicly available, and by eliminating contributions from large organizations or dark-money groups.

Congresswoman Pramila Jayapal of Washington has proposed a constitutional amendment to achieve these goals. "Corporations are not people and money is not speech," she says. "In every election cycle since the disastrous Citizens United decision, we have seen more and more special interest dark money poured into campaigns across the country. My We the People Amendment returns the power to the people by finally ending corporate constitutional rights, reversing Citizens United, and ensuring that our democracy is truly of the people, by the people, and for the people—not corporations."

BRING BACK NONCITIZEN VOTING

For much of American history, noncitizens were allowed to vote in some elections, and a number of cities and states now permit them to vote once again. Anti-immigrant rhetoric has helped fuel a fear of so-called voter fraud, but experts have shown that voting actually increases a sense of community, public safety, and belonging, not only for noncitizens but for all Americans. Today, several municipalities (towns or cities) in California, Maryland, and Vermont allow noncitizens to participate in elections— but most of the nation's twenty-five million noncitizens (including eleven million legal permanent residents) cannot make their voices heard in government.

PROTECT OUR ELECTIONS SYSTEM

A US government review of the 2020 election called it "the most secure in American history."

"There is no evidence," the report continued, "that any voting system deleted or lost votes, changed votes, or was in any way compromised."

Maintaining a safe, secure, and modern voting system is one of the most important things we can do to protect people power in America, especially when so many politicians are urging their followers to reject election outcomes despite the lack of evidence that anything wrong has happened.

After the 2020 election, many states took steps to protect their election systems, and their employees, from politically motivated attacks. But many others remain at risk of falling into the hands of politicians whose only interest is in warping the system for political gain.

WHAT YOU CAN DO

THE MESSAGE OF *REPRESENT* IS THAT IF YOU ARE EIGHTEEN or older, voting in every election is one of the most important things you can do as a citizen of the United States.

Well before every election, it's important to check that your voter registration status is current and to educate yourself about the candidates running for office. Some of the online resources below make this easier than ever.

This first-time voter checklist is a great place to start:

https://www.vote411.org/make-your-plan

There are many other ways to participate in elections, even for people not yet old enough to vote:

SUPPORT VOTER REGISTRATION EFFORTS

All voters must first register before participating in an election. Helping people register increases the number of voters and keeps our democracy healthy. These organizations provide many opportunities for volunteers to support this work:

HeadCount: https://www.headcount.org/volunteer

League of Women Voters: https://www.lwv.org/about-us /membership-local-leagues

Rock the Vote: https://www.rockthevote.org/get-involved /volunteer-with-rock-the-vote

When We All Vote: https://whenweallvote.org/takeaction /volunteer

HELP FIGHT VOTER SUPPRESSION

A number of pro-democracy organizations need volunteers to fight back against efforts to keep people away from the polls:

Common Cause: https://www.mobilize.us/commoncause

Election Protection: https://protectthevote.net

Legal Defense Fund: https://voting.naacpldf.org/voting -rights/prepared-to-vote/volunteer-with-ptv-and-vrd

VoteRiders: https://www.voteriders.org/volunteer

We the Action: https://electionprotection.wetheaction.org

SUPPORT VOTER EDUCATION EFFORTS

Most of the organizations listed in this section provide information to voters about their rights, voter registration, candidates, and Election Day rules. You can help broadcast this information through your own personal networks, your social media, and by distributing flyers in your local community.

SUPPORT A POLITICAL CANDIDATE OR OFFICEHOLDER WHOSE VIEWS YOU AGREE WITH

People running for office need all the help they can get, and usually employ large numbers of volunteers to make phone calls, organize events, fundraise, and more. Using the resources below, you can learn about who is running for office in your area or who represents you already. Most officeholders or candidates have websites with information about how to volunteer.

Ballotpedia: https://ballotpedia.org/Sample_Ballot_Lookup

Common Cause: https://www.commoncause.org/find-your -representative

Legal Defense Fund: https://www.naacpldf.org/research -candidates-state-local-elections

FOR FURTHER INFORMATION ABOUT VOTING-RIGHTS ACTIVISM:

Black Voters Matter Fund: https://blackvotersmatterfund .org/volunteer

League of Women Voters: https://www.lwv.org/blog/5-ways -volunteer-voting-rights

WHAT YOU CAN DO

Mashable: https://mashable.com/article/organizations-get
-out-the-vote-donate

Native American Rights Fund: https://vote.narf.org/native
-american-voting-rights-act-navra

Voto Latino Foundation: https://votolatino.org/takeaction

INFORMATION FOR FIRST-TIME VOTERS:

Common Cause: https://www.commoncause.org/voting-tools

Election Protection/866 Our Vote: https://866ourvote.org

United States Election Assistance Commission: https://www
.eac.gov/voters/register-and-vote-in-your-state

USAGov: https://www.usa.gov/register-to-vote

Vote 411: https://www.vote411.org

Vote.org: https://www.vote.org

VOTING-RIGHTS TIMELINE

1789	1807	1820s–1830s	1870
The US Constitution is ratified. America's founding document gave states the responsibility for establishing voting laws, but did not create a national right to vote for all citizens. Voting is almost entirely limited to white men who own property.	New Jersey passes a law prohibiting women from voting.	Property restrictions for voting are knocked down in most states, making it possible for all free men to vote. At the same time, many states establish laws limiting voting rights to white men only, reversing decades of representation for African Americans.	The Fifteenth Amendment prohibits voting restrictions on the basis of race, protecting the right of Black men to vote in the United States.

VOTING-RIGHTS TIMELINE

1882

The Chinese Exclusion Act prevents people born in China from becoming citizens of the United States.

1884

In the US Supreme Court case *Elk v. Wilkins*, it is decided that Native Americans cannot vote because they are not citizens of the United States.

1889

A poll tax is enacted in Florida, the first of many Southern states requiring fees to be paid before voting, which prevents many African Americans and poor people from registering to vote.

1890

Wyoming becomes the first state since 1807 to fully give women the right to vote. Colorado follows in 1893, along with Utah and Idaho in 1896.

VOTING-RIGHTS TIMELINE

1913

The Seventeenth Amendment to the US Constitution gives voters the power to elect US senators directly. Prior to that, senators were elected by state legislators, in order to create a buffer between the will of the people and this powerful governing body.

1920

The Nineteenth Amendment to the US Constitution guarantees women's right to vote: "The right of citizens of the United States to vote shall not be denied or abridged by the United States or by any State on account of sex."

1924

The Indian Citizenship Act grants citizenship to all Native American people born in the United States.

1943

The Magnuson Act repeals the Chinese Exclusion Act, giving all people of Chinese descent the right to become citizens and vote.

VOTING-RIGHTS TIMELINE

1961	1964	1965	1971
The Twenty-Third Amendment to the US Constitution gives residents of Washington, DC, the right to vote in presidential elections. DC residents are still not represented in the House of Representatives or the Senate.	The Twenty-Fourth Amendment to the Constitution makes poll taxes illegal in federal elections; in 1966, the Supreme Court outlaws poll taxes in state elections as well.	Congress passes the Voting Rights Act, which gave the government special powers to enforce the Fifteenth Amendment and outlawed literacy tests for voting.	The Twenty-Sixth Amendment to the US Constitution lowers the legal voting age from twenty-one to eighteen, partly in response to the hundreds of thousands of young people who served as soldiers in the Vietnam War. "Old enough to fight, old enough to vote" was a popular slogan at this time.

VOTING-RIGHTS TIMELINE

1975

Amendments to the Voting Rights Act require local governments to provide help to non-English speakers in registering and voting.

1993

The National Voter Registration Act—also known as the "motor voter" law—makes it easier for Americans to register to vote, especially when getting a driver's license.

2013

In *Shelby County v. Holder*, the Supreme Court overturns section 4(b) of the Voting Rights Act, which had required states with a history of discrimination to notify the federal government about any changes in voting laws— which was meant to prevent the reemergence of old patterns of voting-rights discrimination in the South.

2021

The US House of Representatives passes the John R. Lewis Voting Rights Advancement Act, which seeks to reverse the effects of *Shelby County v. Holder* and strengthen the ability of all Americans to vote. The act later stalls in the US Senate.

FOR FURTHER READING

For anyone wanting to go deeper into the history of voting rights in America or to understand how voting works (and doesn't work) today, here is our selection of the best books on these subjects for general readers.

Anderson, Carol. *One Person, No Vote: How Voter Suppression Is Destroying Our Democracy*. New York: Bloomsbury, 2018.

Berman, Ari. *Give Us the Ballot: The Modern Struggle for Voting Rights in America*. New York: Picador, 2016.

Daley, David. *Ratf**cked: The True Story Behind the Secret Plan to Steal America's Democracy*. New York: Liveright, 2016.

Dionne, Evette. *Lifting as We Climb: Black Women's Battle for the Ballot Box*. New York: Viking Books for Young Readers, 2022.

DuBois, Ellen Carol. *Suffrage: Women's Long Battle for the Vote*. New York: Simon & Schuster, 2020.

Foner, Eric. *The Second Founding: How the Civil War and Reconstruction Remade the Constitution*. New York: W. W. Norton, 2019.

Jones, Martha S. *Vanguard: How Black Women Broke Barriers, Won the Vote, and Insisted on Democracy for All.* New York: Basic Books, 2021.

Keyssar, Alexander. *The Right to Vote: The Contested History of Democracy in the United States.* Rev. ed. New York: Basic Books, 2009.

Lemay, Kate Clarke, ed. *Votes for Women! A Portrait of Persistence.* Princeton, NJ: Princeton University Press, 2019.

Lichtman, Allan J. *The Embattled Vote in America: From the Founding to the Present.* Cambridge, MA: Harvard University Press, 2018.

Litt, David. *Democracy in One Book or Less: How It Works, Why It Doesn't, and Why Fixing It Is Easier Than You Think.* New York: Ecco, 2020.

Smith, Erin Geiger. *Thank You for Voting: The Maddening, Enlightening, Inspiring Truth About Voting in America.* New York: Harper, 2020.

Waldman, Michael. *The Fight to Vote.* New York: Simon & Schuster, 2022.

Wehle, Kim. *What You Need to Know About Voting and Why.* New York: Harper, 2020.

ONLINE RESOURCES

The following organizations provide reliable, expert information on voting and elections in America:

Brennan Center for Justice: https://www.brennancenter.org

Democracy Docket: https://www.democracydocket.com

League of Women Voters: https://www.lwv.org

Rock the Vote: https://www.rockthevote.org

Voting Rights Lab: https://votingrightslab.org

SOURCE NOTES

PROLOGUE: WHOSE REVOLUTION?

2   "We are endowed with the same faculties": Herbert
     Aptheker, ed., *A Documentary History of the Negro People in
     the United States*, vol. 1, *From Colonial Times to the Civil War*
     (New York: Citadel Press, 1951), 11.

5   "Be it enacted...no person shall vote": "Why Did
     Women Lose the Vote? The Backlash," *When Women Lost
     the Vote*, Museum of the American Revolution exhibit,
     https://www.amrevmuseum.org/virtualexhibits/when
     -women-lost-the-vote-a-revolutionary-story/pages/how
     -did-women-lose-the-vote-the-backlash.

CHAPTER TWO: TWO STEPS BACK

25   "When you have taken from an individual his right to vote":
     Robert Purvis, *Appeal of Forty Thousand Citizens, Threatened
     with Disfranchisement, to the People of Pennsylvania*
     (Philadelphia, 1838).

26   "We have no protection in law": David Ruggles,
     "Kidnapping in the City of New York," *Liberator*, August
     6, 1836, quoted in Ira Berlin, *The Long Emancipation: The*

Demise of Slavery in the United States (Cambridge, MA: Harvard University Press, 2015), 134.

27   "What, to the American slave, is your 4th of July?": Frederick Douglass, "The Meaning of July Fourth for the Negro," in Philip S. Foner, *The Life and Writings of Frederick Douglass*, vol. 2, *Pre–Civil War Decade: 1850–1860* (New York: International, 1950), 192.

CHAPTER THREE: LIBERATION

32   "slavery is not abolished until the black man has the ballot": Frederick Douglass, "Reconstruction, and an Appeal to Impartial Suffrage," *Atlantic*, November 23, 2011.

36   "heart and soul of their freedom": historian Anne C. Bailey, quoted in Eric Foner, *The Second Founding: How the Civil War and Reconstruction Remade the Constitution.* (New York: W. W. Norton and Co., 2019), 94.

37   "The irresistible tendency of modern civilization": *Cong. Globe*, 40th Cong., 3d Sess. 709 (1869), quoted in Foner, *Second Founding*, 99.

38   "the most important event that has occurred since the nation came into life": James D. Richardson, ed., *A Compilation of the Messages and Papers of the Presidents, 1789–1897*, vol. 7 (Washington, DC, 1899), 56, quoted in Foner, *Second Founding*, 111.

38   "a greater revolution than that of 1776": "Reconstruction Completed—The New Dispensation and the Political Parties of the Day," *New York Herald*, April 1, 1870, quoted in Foner, *Second Founding*, 111.

38   "Never was revolution more complete": Frederick Douglass, "At Last, at Last, the Black Man Has a Future: An Address Delivered in Albany, New York, on April 22, 1870," Frederick Douglass Papers Digital Edition, https://frederickdouglass papersproject.com/s/digitaledition/item/17841.

CHAPTER FOUR: SUFFRAGE

45   "We hold these truths to be self-evident: that all men and women are created equal": "Declaration of Sentiments," in *Report of the Woman's Rights Convention, Held at Seneca Falls, N.Y., July 19th and 20th, 1848* (Rochester, NY, 1848), 7, quoted in Ellen Carol DuBois, *Suffrage: Women's Long Battle for the Vote* (New York: Simon & Schuster, 2020), 305.

48   "to secure Equal Rights to all American citizens": *The American Equal Rights Association and the Battle for the Vote*, online exhibit at the New-York Historical Society, August 31, 2023, https://www.nyhistory.org/blogs/the -american-equal-rights-association-and-the-battle.

50   "unlettered and unwashed": Elizabeth Cady Stanton, "Address to Anniversary of American Equal Rights Association," *Revolution* 3, no. 19 (May 13, 1869): 289–92.

50   "I must say that I do not see how any one can pretend": "The May Anniversaries in New York and Brooklyn," in *History of Woman Suffrage*, eds. Elizabeth Cady Stanton, Susan B. Anthony, and Matilda Joslyn Gage, vol. 2, *1861–1876* (Rochester, NY, 1881), 382, quoted in Michael Waldman, *The Fight to Vote* (New York: Simon & Schuster, 2016), 69.

CHAPTER FIVE: BETRAYAL

57   A discussion of the original Colfax Massacre historical marker can be found in Tom Barber and Jeff Crawford, "Removing the White Supremacy Marker at Colfax, Louisiana: A 2021 Success Story," *Journal of the Civil War Era*, July 6, 2021, https://www.journalofthecivilwarera .org/2021/07/removing-the-white-supremacy-marker-at -colfax-louisiana-a-2021-success-story.

58   "Every Democrat must feel honor bound to control the vote": South Carolina "Red Shirts" Battle Plan, quoted in

SOURCE NOTES

Facing History and Ourselves, https://www.facinghistory
.org/sites/default/files/2022-07/South_Carolina_Red_Shirts
_Battle%20Plan_1876.pdf.

59   "Then it was that we stuffed ballot boxes": Wade Hampton,
quoted in "It's Not Just the Flag: South Carolina Officially
Celebrates Hero of White Death Squads," *Slate*, June 22, 2015.

CHAPTER SIX: DOWNFALL

66   "The great question of the Elective Franchise": Michael
Perman, *Struggle for Mastery: Disfranchisement in the South,
1888–1908* (Chapel Hill: University of North Carolina
Press, 2001), 178.

67   "Discrimination! Why, that is precisely what we propose":
*Report of the Proceedings and Debates of the Constitutional
Convention, State of Virginia: Held in the City of Richmond
June 12, 1901, to June 26, 1902*, vol. 2 (Richmond, VA:
Hermitage Press, 1906), 3076, quoted in Perman, *Struggle
for Mastery*, 221.

69   "Question: Does enumeration affect": "Alabama Voter
Literacy Test Documents, circa 1965," Georgia State
University Digital Collections, https://digitalcollections
.library.gsu.edu/digital/collection/AFLCIO/id/22389.

69   "Question: How does the Constitution of Georgia
provide": Quoted in Today in Georgia History, https://
www.todayingeorgiahistory.org/tih-georgia-day/georgias
-literacy-test.

CHAPTER SEVEN: THE FLAME

81   "If the Democratic party wants to catch up with China":
"Ask Suffrage Plank," *York (PA) Dispatch*, June 14, 1912,
quoted in Catherine D. Cahill, *Recasting the Vote: How*

SOURCE NOTES

Women of Color Changed the Suffrage Movement (Chapel Hill: University of North Carolina Press, 2020), 40.

81 "All women are recognized in New York, excepting Chinese women": Marie Jenney Howe, "The Tables Turned," *Woman Voter*, May 1912, 13, quoted in Cahill, *Recasting the Vote*, 32.

84 "Always, sitting there listening to my countrymen": "Ah Tie, Once a Slave Girl, the First Chinese Woman to Vote in America for a President," *Daily News* (San Francisco), May 20, 1912, quoted in Lia Dun, "Interpreter, Voter, and Pinball Aficionado," Immigrant Voices, Angel Island Immigration Station Foundation, https://www.immigrant -voices.aiisf.org/stories-by-author/807-interpreter-voter-and -pinball-aficionado.

85 "My first vote?": "Ah Tie," *Daily News*, May 20, 1912.

87 "Well, if the mere mention of votes for women has that effect": quoted in Steve Thornton, "A Feeling of Solidarity: Labor Unions and Suffragists Team Up," *Connecticut History*, March 7, 2022, https://connecticuthistory.org/a -feeling-of-solidarity-labor-unions-and-suffragists-team-up.

CHAPTER EIGHT: THE STORYTELLER

93 "What caused them to stoop and look under the bed I do not know": Zitkala-Sa, "The School Days of an Indian Girl," in *American Indian Stories* (Washington, DC: Hayworth, 1921), 55–56.

96 "all persons of one-half or more Indian ancestry": William Willard, in "Zitkala Sa: A Woman Who Would Be Heard!," *Wicazo Sa Review* 1, no. 1 (Spring 1985): 14, quoted in Tadeusz Lewandowski, *Red Bird, Red Power: The Life and Legacy of Zitkala-Ša* (Norman: University of Oklahoma Press, 2016), 167–68.

96 "legalized robbery": Lewandowski, *Red Bird, Red Power*, 167.

SOURCE NOTES

CHAPTER NINE: SENTINELS

99   "Where are all the people?": Michael Waldman, *The Fight to Vote* (New York: Simon & Schuster, 2016), 119.

102   "This is the time to fight": Inez Milholland quoted in "Recreating a Suffragist's Campaign Through the American West," *Smithsonian*, July 2020, https://www.smithsonianmag.com/history/recreating-inez-milholland-boissevain-barnstorming-tour-american-west-180975173.

103   "Mr. President, how long must women wait": Meredith Mendelsohn, "She Was More Than Just the 'Most Beautiful Suffragist,'" *New York Times*, August 19, 2020, https://www.nytimes.com/2020/08/19/arts/design/inez-milholland-suffragist.html.

104   "We are being imprisoned": Doris Stevens, *Jailed for Freedom* (New York: Liveright, 1920), 214, quoted in Waldman, *Fight to Vote*, 122.

106   "We had an enormous bell": Kate Clarke Lemay, ed., *Votes for Women: A Portrait of Persistence* (Princeton, NJ: Princeton University Press, 2019), 214.

CHAPTER TEN: SIDELINED

111   "Our peculiar status in this country": Martha Jones, *Vanguard: How Black Women Broke Barriers, Won the Vote, and Insisted on Equality for All* (New York: Basic Books, 2020), 154.

114   "the Indians aren't allowed to have a voice": Robert Grady, "Henry Mitchell, Indian Canoe Maker," Maine, 1938–39, American Life Histories: Manuscripts from the Federal Writers' Project, 1936 to 1940, Library of Congress, https://www.loc.gov/item/wpalh000609/.

SOURCE NOTES

CHAPTER ELEVEN: FREEDOM

117 "We want only one thing, primarily": C. E. Johnson to James Weldon Johnson, April 19, 1920, box C-388, NAACP, quoted in Neil R. McMillen, *Dark Journey: Black Mississippians in the Age of Jim Crow* (Urbana: University of Illinois Press, 1989), 55.

122 "I had never heard, until 1962, that black people": Fannie Lou Hamer, interview by Neil McMillen, April 14, 1972, transcript, Center for Oral History and Cultural Heritage, University of Southern Mississippi, https://usm.access.preservica.com/uncategorized /IO_886eddaa-ca3f-4173-968f-43fe6aebf542.

123 "You know the ballot is good": Fannie Lou Hamer, "I Don't Mind My Light Shining," in *The Speeches of Fannie Lou Hamer: To Tell It Like It Is*, eds. Maegan Parker Brooks and Davis W. Houck (Oxford: University Press of Mississippi, 2011), 5.

125 "We want to register, to become first-class citizens": Fannie Lou Hamer, "Testimony Before the Credentials Committee at the Democratic National Convention, Atlantic City, New Jersey, August 22, 1964," in Brooks and Houck, *Speeches*, 45.

126 "this act flows from a clear": President Lyndon B. Johnson, quoted in "August 6, 1965: Remarks on the Signing of the Voting Rights Act," UVA Miller Center, Presidential Speeches, https://millercenter.org/the-presidency/presidential -speeches/august-6-1965-remarks-signing-voting-rights-act.

126 "The right to vote is precious": John Lewis (@repjohnlewis), X, July 26, 2016, 3:39 PM, https://x.com /repjohnlewis/status/758023941998776321.

CHAPTER TWELVE: THE BLACK PANTHER

130 "Now is the time!": Hasan Kwame Jeffries, *Bloody Lowndes: Civil Rights and Black Power in Alabama's Black Belt* (New York: New York University Press, 2009), 192.

132 "when you have a situation where the community is 80 percent black": Jeffries, *Bloody Lowndes*, 149.

133 "We just couldn't keep bringing": Jeffries, 78.

134 "The Black Panther is an animal": Jeffries, 152.

135 "I pulled that lever till the black cat howled": Terence Cannon, "Lowndes County Candidates Lose, but Black Panther Strong," *The Movement*, December 1966, quoted in Jeffries, 203.

CHAPTER THIRTEEN: VOICE

140 "the biggest voter registration organization": Juan A. Sepúlveda Jr., *The Life and Times of Willie Velásquez: Su Voto Es Su Voz* (Houston: Arte Público Press, 2003), 133.

140 "Su voto es su voz": Sepúlveda, *Willie Velásquez*, 17.

142 "If we [Mexican Americans] started a revolution": Sepúlveda, 147.

144 "There is no question that we are participating": Sepúlveda, 161.

145 "qué bonito es el nuevo mundo": Sepúlveda, 384.

CHAPTER FOURTEEN: DIRTY TRICKS

150 "changed the weather in the room when she walked in": Ari Berman, *Give Us the Ballot: The Modern Struggle for Voting Rights in America* (New York: Picador, 2016), 136.

151 "Just being a voter in Pickens County": *Extension of the Voting Rights Act: Hearings Before the Subcommittee on Civil and Constitutional Rights of the Committee on the Judiciary, House of Representatives*, pt. 2 (Washington: Government Printing Office, 1982), 1566.

153 "Against all odds, we might find a way": Avi Holzman and Jimmy Hu, "Civil Rights Activist Michelle Alexander Discusses Structural Racism," *Student Life*, Washington University, Saint Louis, March 1, 2023, https://www

.studlife.com/news/2023/03/01/civil-rights-activist-michelle -alexander-discusses-structural-racism.

154 "I wasn't alone in this": Angela Caputo, Geoff Hing, and Johnny Kauffman, "After the Purge: How a Massive Voter Purge in Georgia Affected the 2018 Election," APM Reports, October 29, 2019, https://www.apmreports.org /story/2019/10/29/georgia-voting-registration-records -removed.

155 "It's kind of mind-blowing": Caputo, Hing, and Kauffman, "After the Purge."

158 "throwing out preclearance when it has worked and is continuing to work": *Shelby County v. Holder*, 570 U.S. 529, 590 (2013) (Ginsburg, J., dissenting).

CHAPTER FIFTEEN: DIVISIONS

161 "it's like [lawmakers] don't even know we are here": Neelam Bohra, "Congressional Gerrymandering by Texas Republicans Cut Out the Heart of Houston's Asian Community," *Texas Tribune*, November 22, 2021, https://www.texastribune.org /2021/11/22/texas-redistricting-congressional-asian.

162 "Who is going to stand up for our community?": Bohra, "Congressional Gerrymandering."

162 "because poll workers could not read their names": Bohra, "Congressional Gerrymandering."

163 "the toxic lead pipes": Kathay Feng, "How Fair Voting Maps Turned Out Voters in the Midterm Elections," *Boulder Daily Camera*, November 18, 2022, https://www.dailycamera .com/2022/11/18/guest-opinion-kathay-feng-how-fair-voting -maps-turned-out-voters-in-the-midterm-elections.

168 "It means basically that the whole constitutional notion": David Daley, *Ratf**cked: The True Story Behind the Secret Plan to Steal America's Democracy* (New York: Liveright, 2016), xxi.

169   "Everything hangs in the balance": Feng, "How Fair Voting Maps Turned Out Voters."

169   "We are in a time of history": Bohra, "Congressional Gerrymandering."

CHAPTER SIXTEEN: BIG MONEY, BIG PROBLEMS

178   "You get a Rolodex; you go outside the building": Alan K. Simpson, in Chris Lee, "HBO's John Oliver Exposes the Awful and Absurd Ways Congress Members Raise Money," Yahoo Finance, April 4, 2016, https://finance.yahoo.com /news/hbo-john-oliver-exposes-absurd-130305608.html.

178   "If you want your voice to be heard": Norah O'Donnell, "Are Members of Congress Becoming Telemarketers?," *60 Minutes*, CBS News, April 24, 2016, https://www.cbsnews .com/news/60-minutes-are-members-of-congress-becoming -telemarketers/.

178   "If there's a person in the Senate who": Ian Donnis, "Whitehouse Blames 'Dark Money' for Why He Raised So Much for '18 Campaign," The Public's Radio, April 23, 2019, https://thepublicsradio.org/article/whitehouse-blames -dark-money-for-his-big-spend-on-18-campaign.

179   "the decision has helped reinforce": Tim Lau, "Citizens United Explained," Brennan Center for Justice, December 12, 2019, https://www.brennancenter.org/our-work /research-reports/citizens-united-explained?ref=foreverwars .ghost.io.

CHAPTER SEVENTEEN: TRUTH AND LIES

185   "a disease that is spreading": Larry Jacobs, quoted in Amy Gardner, "A Majority of GOP Nominees Deny or Question the 2020 Election Results," *Washington Post*, October 12, 2022, https://www.washingtonpost.com/nation/2022/10/06 /elections-deniers-midterm-elections-2022.

SOURCE NOTES

188 "And we fight": "Transcript of Trump's Speech at Rally Before US Capitol Riot," Associated Press, January 13, 2021, https://apnews.com/article/election-2020-joe-biden-donald-trump-capitol-siege-media-e79eb5164613d6718e9f4502eb471f27.

189 "We were told to pull out our gas masks": Chris Daniels, "'I Remember Every Detail': Rep. Jayapal Reflects on Capitol Riot One Year Later," *King 5 News*, January 6, 2022, https://www.king5.com/article/news/nation-world/jayapal-reflects-capitol-riot-one-year-later/281-34679137-bd58-4fcf-bbc3-cec1703152d5.

189 "There was a very real fear that these people": "'There Was a Very Real Fear That We Would Not Make It Out': Rep. Pramila Jayapal on Her Escape from the Capitol Riot," *Deconstructed*, podcast, The Intercept, January 15, 2021, https://theintercept.com/2021/01/15/deconstructed-jayapal-capitol-escape.

190 "Beginning election night and continuing through Jan. 6": Alan Feuer, "Key Findings from the Jan. 6 Committee's Report, Annotated," *New York Times*, December 19, 2022, https://www.nytimes.com/2022/12/19/us/politics/jan-6-committee-key-findings.html.

191 "it was a violent insurrection": Senator Mitch McConnell, quoted in "Senator Mitch McConnell Rebukes RNC, Calls Jan. 6 'Violent Insurrection'," *PBS News Hour*, February 8, 2022, https://www.pbs.org/newshour/politics/sen-mitch-mcconnell-rebukes-rnc-calls-jan-6-violent-insurrection.

193 "I told them—of course it should be safe": Barbara Sprunt, "'They Thought They Were Going to Die': Raskin Recounts Family's Experience on Jan. 6," NPR, February 9, 2021, https://www.npr.org/sections/trump-impeachment-trial-live-updates/2021/02/09/965932072/they-thought-they-were-going-to-die-raskin-recounts-familys-experience-on-jan-6.

SOURCE NOTES

193   "There's a difference between fact and fiction":
Jamie Raskin, interview by Judy Woodruff,
PBS NewsHour, June 10, 2022, https://www.pbs
.org/newshour/show/rep-raskin-on-what-the-jan-6
-committee-accomplished-in-the-first-public-hearing.

EPILOGUE: MORE IS MORE

196   "Voting rights is not just some other issue": Stephen
Neukam, "Warnock: 'We Can't Afford to Give Up on
Voting Rights,'" *The Hill,* January 16, 2023, https://thehill
.com/blogs/blog-briefing-room/3815211-warnock-we-cant
-afford-to-give-up-on-voting-rights.

PEOPLE-POWER IDEAS

205   "one of the ways in which to get the consent": Miles
Rapoport, quoted in "Miles Rapoport on How We Can
Achieve Universal Voting," *Democracy Paradox,* podcast,
March 29, 2022, https://democracyparadox.com/2022/03/29
/miles-rapoport-on-how-we-can-achieve-universal-voting.

206   "Corporations are not people": Rep. Pramila Jayapal,
quoted in "Jayapal Introduces Constitutional Amendment
to Reverse *Citizens United,*" April 4, 2023, press release,
https://jayapal.house.gov/2023/04/04/jayapal-introduces
-constitutional-amendment-to-reverse-citizens-united.

207   "the most secure in American history": Cybersecurity
and Infrastructure Security Agency, "Joint Statement
from Elections Infrastructure Government Coordinating
Council & the Election Infrastructure Sector Coordinating
Executive Committees," press release, November 12, 2020,
https://www.cisa.gov/news-events/news/joint-statement
-elections-infrastructure-government-coordinating-council
-election.

INDEX

NOTE: Page numbers in *italics* refer to photographs.

INDEX

INDEX

INDEX

Guinn v. United States
(grandfather clauses),
70–71

H

Hamer, Fannie Lou, 115,
122–25, 152
Hampton, Wade, III, 58–60
Harvard Law School, 150
Haudenosaunee (Iroquois), 95
Hayes, Rutherford B., 60–61
Hispanic voters, 139–45
House of Representatives
election of 1824, 14, 15, 16
expanding the, 202
gag rule, 22
gerrymandering, 163–69
Howard-Shaw, Anna, 81
Howard University, 130
Hulett, John, 136

I

immigrants, 73–74, 75. *See also*
Chinese immigrants and
citizens
Indian Citizenship Act of 1924,
113–14, 215
inequality, 3, 9, 10, 13, 43
Inglis, Bob, 171–72
interracial marriages, 19, 84

J

Jackson, Andrew, 13–14, 96
election of 1824, 14, 15, 16
election of 1828, 16–17, 21
Jacobs, Larry, 185
January 6 riot. *See* Capitol riot
of 2021
Jayapal, Pramila, 189, 206–7
Jim Crow, 72, 86, 117, 118,
141, 151
John R. Lewis Voting Rights
Advancement Act of 2021,
195–96, 217

Johnson, Andrew, 32, 33
Johnson, Lyndon, 125–26
Juan Crow, 141

K

Kellogg, William Pitt, 55
Koch Industries, 172
Ku Klux Klan (KKK), 54, 56

L

League of Women Voters, 211,
220
Lee, George W., 120
Lee, Mabel Ping-Hua, 79–80,
81, 85, 86, 112
Legal Defense Fund, 210, 211
Leung, Tye, 83–85
Lewis, John, 125, 126, 130, 140,
194, 195–96
Lewis Voting Rights
Advancement Act of 2021,
195–96, 217
Lincoln, Abraham, 33
literacy tests, 68–69, 70–71, 73,
75, 118, 140–41, 216
Liuzzo, Viola, 129
Lovejoy, Elijah, 23
Lowndes County, Alabama,
129–37
Lowndes County Freedom
Organization, *128*, 134–36
lynchings, 53–54, 111

M

McConnell, Mitch, 191
McEnery, John, 55
Magnuson Act of 1943, 215
mail-in ballots, 150, 181, 203
mandatory voting, 205
Maptitude, 165–67, 205–6
Mexican American voters,
139–45
Michel, Robert, 178
Milholland, Inez, 101–4

INDEX

Mississippi, 23, 62, 66, 71, 111, 118–19, 120, 123–25
Mississippi Freedom Democratic Party, 124–25
Mississippi "freedom vote," 123
money in politics. *See* campaign finance
Montgomery bus boycott, 119
Moore, Joe Ella, *116*, 126–27
Mott, Lucretia, 44, 48, 115

N

National American Woman Suffrage Association (NAWSA), *76*, 81
National Association for the Advancement of Colored People (NAACP), 97, 117–18, 149–50
National Association of Colored Women (NACW), 110–12
National Hispanic Voter Registration Campaign, 144–45
National Voter Registration Act of 1993, 217
National Woman's Party, *98*, 103–7, 114–15
Native American boarding schools, 91–92, 93–94
Native American Rights Fund, 212
Native Americans, 4–5, 75, 89–97, 113–14, 214, 215
New Jersey Constitution, 4, 5–6, 213
New Jim Crow, The (Alexander), 152–53
New York City Suffrage Parades, 78–79, 81, 86
night riders, 53–54, 184
Nineteenth Amendment, 106–7, 109–10, 215
noncitizen voting ("alien suffrage"), 73, 207

non-English speakers, voting assistance for, 203, 217
Norman, Hyunja, 161–62
North Carolina, 67, 206

O

Obama, Barack, 49, 165, 166
Occoquan Workhouse, 104–5
Old Indian Legends (Zitkála-Šá), 93–94
"one person, one vote," 162, 173
Ornstein, Norman, 168

P

partisan gerrymandering. *See* gerrymandering
Paul, Alice, 77, 99–101, 103–6, 109, 111
"pauper laws," 73–74
Pence, Mike, 172, 188–89
people-power ideas, 201–8
Pickens County, Alabama, 150–51
Planter, USS, 29–30
poll taxes, *64*, 68, 70–71, 75, 118, 140–41, 214, 216
Pomeroy, Samuel, 37
popular vote, 15, 167–68, 187, 201–2
preclearance, 147, 158
property qualification, 4, 11–13, 213
Purvis, Robert, *18*, 19–26, 38

Q

Qing dynasty, 79

R

racism, 22, 48–49, 50–51, 53–54, 57, 59, 66–67, 71, 120–21, 152–53. *See also* anti-Chinese racism
Radical Reconstruction, 34–35, 61

INDEX

INDEX

KK OTTESEN

DR. MICHAEL ERIC DYSON

is an award-winning and *New York Times* bestselling author of over twenty books, a widely celebrated professor, a prominent public intellectual, an ordained Baptist minister, and a noted political analyst. A native of Detroit, Michigan, he currently lives in Nashville, Tennessee. He invites you to follow him on X @michaeledyson and at Facebook.com/michaelericdyson.

MOLLY GLASGOW

MARC FAVREAU is the director

of editorial programs at the New Press, the acclaimed author of *Crash, Spies*, and *Attacked!*, and coauthor (with Michael Eric Dyson) of *Unequal: A Story of America*, a finalist for the YALSA Award for Excellence in Nonfiction for Young Adults. He lives in Martha's Vineyard, Massachusetts.